CW01214252

REVIEWS OF THE ORIGINAL EDITION OF FRANK BINDER'S
A Journey in England

MANCHESTER GUARDIAN: "The claim of the publishers to 'individuality' is assuredly justified in this re-discovery of England from a fresh view point ... No doubt can be expressed as to the further claim to distinction of style as displayed in Mr Binder's volume."

SUNDAY TIMES: "Another 'Eothen' ... engaging and provocative."

Miss Adcock in OVERSEAS: "Deliciously amusing and refreshing, glittering with rapier-like truths, so deftly handled that they pick rather than wound, even when directed against our own vanity."

THE SPECTATOR: "Chester and Ely and Lincoln and Stratford and Oxford, to say nothing of Sheffield and Liverpool... He moralizes about each in a pleasant Sterne-like fashion, walking among these historic jewels with a delicate Agag gait."

PUNCH: "The reader will discover a certain stimulation in his attitude towards England ... a pretty pedestrian and memorable observer."

NEW STATESMAN: "Few writers are as careful of their work as Mr Binder is, and for that alone we should be grateful to him."

ENGLISH REVIEW: "He is a pagan obsessed with the futility of his short stay on earth."

LONDON MERCURY: "It is a rare book, discovering not England alone, but also much of Mr Binder's engaging personality."

EVERYMAN: "The book is a charming, intimate affair that

makes very pleasant reading."

A JOURNEY IN ENGLAND

FRANK BINDER

Copyright © Elsie Binder 2013

All rights reserved. No part of this publication may be reproduced, stored in a retrieval system, or transmitted, in any form or by any means, electronic, mechanical, photocopying, recording or otherwise, without the prior permission of both the copyright owners and the publisher.

Elsie Binder has asserted the late Frank Binder's right to be identified as the author of this work in accordance with the Copyright, Designs and Patents Act 1988.

Originally published by Eric Partridge Ltd at
The Scholartis Press in 1931

This second edition published in Great Britain in 2013
by
Farthings Publishing
8/1 Avenue Victoria
SCARBOROUGH
YO11 2QB
UK
http://www.Farthings-Publishing.com

Cover design by John Roberts
Top Floor Studio, Woodbridge. Suffolk

ISBN 978-1-4466-0665-0

December 2013 (h)

Dedication

Dedicated to the memory of the late Frank Binder (1893 – 1962)

Frank Binder was a much loved and respected teacher at Scarborough High School for Boys from 1940 to 1960. He taught French and German, and, as a passionate lover of chess, passed on his talents to hundreds of schoolboys.

Acknowledgements

Grateful thanks are due to Elsie Binder, for permission to re-publish this manuscript, last published in 1931.

Also by Frank Binder
Published works:

1932 *Dialectics or the Tactics of Thinking*
Eric Partridge Ltd at The Scholartis Press

2010 *Sown with Corn*
Farthings Publishing

2012 Second edition retitled
Their Cemetery Sown with Corn
Pen & Sword Books

Unpublished works:
The Principles of Controversy
The Wisdoms of Ramadan (Science fiction)

CONTENTS

Chapter		Page
	INTRODUCTION by Michael Rines	9
1	MY DIARY	15
2	FROM BONN TO THE HOOK OF HOLLAND	22
3	TO ELY WITH THOUGHTS ON ELY CATHEDRAL	38
4	PETERBOROUGH AND OTHER MATTERS	50
5	TO LINCOLN WITH PESSIMIST REFLECTIONS	61
6	SOMETHING OF LINCOLN	68
7	SOMETHING OF SARCASM (SHEFFIELD AND LIVERPOOL)	81
8	CHESTER	96
9	STRATFORD-ON-AVON	109
10	LEAMINGTON AND WARWICK	118
11	WARWICK CASTLE WITH CERTAIN THOUGHTS ON ART	127
12	KENILWORTH	140
13	OXFORD	150
14	ALONG THE TOWING PATH TO READING	162
15	TO MARLOW WITH FURTHER ROMANTIC REFLECTIONS	173
16	A CLOSE SUBJECT AND AN OPEN DISCUSSION	189
17	DIGRESSIONS FROM THE TOWING PATH	194
18	THE LAST PHASE	205
19	CONCLUSION	218

INTRODUCTION by Michael Rines

A JOURNEY IN ENGLAND

Frank Binder's Classic

Frank Binder's *A Journey in England* was first published, to critical acclaim, in 1932. It was also lauded in Eric Partridge's authoritative reference book on English language and literature, *Usage and Abusage,* still in print under the Penguin Reference imprint (See references under 'Alliteration' and 'Style'). The book describes in glorious prose a tour of parts of England by train and on foot, starting with his journey from Bonn, where he was a distinguished lecturer at the university from 1921 to 1933, before being driven out by the Nazis. The book is based on lectures to his students.

In *A Journey in England* Binder crosses the North German Plain to Ostend before landing in Harwich. He goes on by train to see the great churches and other historic buildings at Ely, Peterborough, Lincoln, Liverpool, Chester, Stratford-on-Avon, Leamington and Warwick, then on foot through Kenilworth, Oxford and Thames towns and villages such as Reading, Maidenhead, Bray, Stoke Poges, Windsor and Runnymede, finally hitching a lift into London.

Journey is not, however, a travelogue, and his descriptions of the historic towns and buildings are couched not in architectural terms but reflect rather the emotions and philosophical thoughts they arouse in him. Moreover, he is as interested in the people he meets as in the historic buildings, from a bargee on the canal at Lincoln to the landlord of an inn on the Thames towpath.

The book is, indeed, as much a vehicle for Binder's philosophy as it is a travel book. More than that, it is a literary treasure, with superb imagery, alliteration, assonance, aphorisms and antithesis woven into the writing.

Take, for instance, his first impressions on emerging from Ely railway station. (Page 43):

'So this was Ely! And I who had in fancy been communing in the chaste asceticism of the Cathedral close, or moving along the avenued approach of spacious beech trees, ancestral elms and stately cedars, saw nothing else ahead of me but a very beery and unbeatific public house, which, like a sort of sodden end of a Saturday afternoon, appeared to be propped up amid other dwellings as dubious and unsabbatarian as the pub itself. ... somehow or other I found myself slumming it through Ely, looking neither to the right nor to the left, but having the impression of a litter of low-browed houses which hovelled on either side of the road.'

His conversion of nouns into verbs ('avenued' and 'hovelled'), which works so well in this passage, is a regular feature of his writing.

Binder is able to conjure up in a single appropriate word the most vivid and accurate pictures, as in the use of 'penitentials' and 'upholstered' in the following passage:

'Now there was little to be seen in the window-display of that photographer's shop. In fact there was nothing else but a spread of poorly parochial portraits, weedy wedding parties, children for confirmation, father in his Sunday penitentials, and the like, most of them with very upholstered expressions and in over-obvious and plebian poses ...'

Again, though there are many solemn and philosophical passages in the book, Binder could be eminently practical – and humorous – too. He recounts how he gave some advice to a student having difficulty in packing his bags to go back to England from Germany:

'I just whispered one word in that young Englishman's ear .... Rolling! ROLLING! ... We seized those suits, and hanging on either end with the struggling grimness of a tug-of-war we rolled them into the compass and consistency of lead pencils. My word, no slackness there was found! You could have slipped his shirts into a test-tube, you could have threaded a needle with his drawers, you could – with luck and in the dark – have paraded the whole job-lot as a bunch of asparagus, blazers, pyjamas, handkerchiefs and socks, all stretched as tight as a banjo string.'

Again, describing his visit to the church at Stoke Poges, he wrote

'The vicar whom I visited was very kind, but certainly not a man of elegiac appearance, of country character, or of churchyard associations. He was young and athletic, and I soon discovered that in Stoke Poges the knell of parting day was less regarded than the toot of his approaching Ford.'

Such passages can be contrasted with much that is more solemn, and Binder had something of a preoccupation with death, which stemmed from the fact that he was, as he described himself, 'a poor pagan'. He therefore had no belief in an afterlife, and his view that we are all, no matter how eminent in life, equal in death, leads logically for him to a disrespect of pretension. During his visit to Lincoln, he came upon 'a gloomy compound, girt in by embattled walls' where low headstones marked the graves of poor people who had been hanged on the castle gallows. (Page 65). He contrasts it with a passage about the burial of the Duke of Monmouth in Macaulay's *History of England.*

The Duke had been buried in the Tower of London, and Macaulay had written 'there is no sadder spot than that little cemetery', and then took note of the many eminent men who met their death on that scaffold, and were buried in that tragic vault. Binder comments, in a passage which provides several examples of his brilliant of use of antithesis:

'Notable names they are of historical interest and of illustrious association, names whose soaring ascendancy is in calamitous contrast to their fall. But humility has its tragedies no less deep, and this burial spot of those who went down with dirty hands and in darkness to their graves has a sadness beyond that of the Tower. For there is no aristocracy in grief, no privilege of purple in the ache of the heart, and though certain blood may plume itself on its blueness, common salt is the scalding quality of all tears. The characters of Macaulay's rhetorical parade had drunk of sweeter cups in life. Their lips touched bitterness only in the last hours. But in Lincoln lie those to whom the cup of bitterness was a daily portion and a birthright, who perhaps had known no other pleasure but freedom from pain, and who never even lived in the twilight of hope before entering the ignoble light of despair. Theirs was the mere shaking of the olive tree of life, the niggard gleaning of the grapes when the full-blooded vintage was over, and their passage in death was from ashes to sackcloth, and from dust to dishonour and dirt.'

This extract is a particularly good demonstration of the way Binder uses antithesis to create rhythm and colour. For instance, in the first sentence, there is the contrast between 'soaring ascendancy' and 'calamitous fall'. Then the sentence beginning 'For there is no aristocracy in grief' has three memorable and effortlessly linked aphorisms, which manage at the same time to be three linked examples of antithesis. There is also liberal use of assonance and alliteration, all in this one sentence. Writing it must have taken a lot of thought, a lot of time and a lot of polishing, but it never feels laboured.

Towards the end of the book he describes how he writes. 'I have a sense of symmetry, a passion for form. I never write without rhythm, without pondering and playing with the balance of syllables and sounds. I am nothing if not musical. I admire a measure in all things.' The result is a prose that is both poetic and musical; blank verse without the verse, poetic prose perhaps. It should not be judged by the same standards as other prose, but more as a unique medium of its own.

He confesses that he does not have the temperament to write in the style expected in a diary, and on the other hand doubts his ability to write a classic. What he boasts of is patience, 'the unflinching patience that can ... resolutely refuse every first impulse and dourly endure attendance on second thoughts.' However, this does not mean he never had doubts when 'lingering overlong on elegancies of expression, on the lilts of language, and on the loveliness of alliteration'.

Journey got good reviews, in publications such as the *Sunday Times*, the *Manchester Guardian*, *The Spectator*, the *New Statesman* and *Punch*, but they did not stop it from being forgotten. Prophetically, in view of the unfair failure of many of his contemporaries to recognise him in his lifetime, he concludes that 'it is a precarious prosperity that comes of embarking the spirit on the instability of syllables and sounds.'

Binder fled from Nazi Germany in 1937, became a much respected language teacher at the Scarborough Boys High School and died in obscurity in 1962. However, he has at last achieved recognition, albeit posthumously. His book *Sown With Corn,* written in the late 1940s about life in a Rhineland village during the rise of the Nazis, was at last published three years ago on a limited scale by Farthings Publishing and has been hailed by leading historians in both the UK and Germany as of great historical importance. Its reception has been such that a second edition has been published under the revised title *Their Cemetery Sown with Corn* by Pen & Sword Books.

CHAPTER ONE

My Diary

I suppose there is no type of literature more big with promise and none more fraught with failure than a diary, none which all have such ambitions to plan, so many the common sense to neglect, and so few the ability to perform. For it is not easy to be intimate, not easy to preserve the privacies when one has put swing-doors on the soul, and made a public bar-room of one's heart. I like to peep into my own penetralia, but the peep must not be public: I like to air my linen however lamentable, but not on the king's highway. Indeed the little dignity that I have would hardly survive the deep domestic drops of a common confession, which, however courageous the cause, could only be crude in its effects. And yet a diary of one's own is most revealing reading. We are all glad to dip into the lilliputian past, to rummage amid unmarketable memories, and to brood over the diurnal details of long ago. How many of us have not entertained the prosperous ambition of writing such pleasing bagatelle, and of embalming the idle litter of our idle days in the scrap amber of lead-pencil prose? And how many of us have not collected on the very first day the straw and stubble of the small talk we have heard, have not skipped the sentences and recorded the commas of life, written our rigid report of nothing in particular, with thoughts of Pepys, and with hopes perhaps of a halo in after years? It is a private truism of everyone, no less than a public confession of my own. I have written many such. The first day was literature, or something very like it, and I lapped my soul in the lily illusion that it would always be so,—for the next day, for the day after that, and for many days to come. But the second day came and went, and literature went with it, and I saw the sun go down on my wrath and my wretchedness with no prospect of an aurora for the morning. And from that hour my diary became a nightmare. Literature went, even journalese went, my rhetorical roses withered, my flowers of fancy famished away, the wastrel weeds of Whitechapel, the brambles and briars of Billingsgate overran the page, till on the seventh day of my creation I careered into a chaos, so void and without form, that I dreaded the thought of a Fiat Lux and let darkness brood in dark places for ever more. I was left with a log-book, a tetrachordon of four trumpery items, —what I had for breakfast, what I had for dinner, what I had for supper, and—the price! Such have been my diaries of the past, diaries that tapered off in interest as a pyramid from its base, diaries that began in an equatorial downpour of inspiration and ended like a tiny Nile which flowed across the desert page, whilst all around the lone and level sands of unfilled margins stretched far away.

The hopes of fools are proverbially the despairs of the wise, and mine, though I admit it, were very hardy, such as could wait for the consolation of Israel and keep up expectations for a seventh monarchy when those for a fifth had been long relinquished. I took courage from many things, and reflected that man is born only for glimpses of glory, that youth is a breath, spring a passing blush, and that noonday simply comes and goes with the tick of it. I had just to wait for the hour, I reasoned, bide the times and seasons which were appointed for all things, not to buttonhole the principalities and powers and to dun my destiny every daily day with a diary, but to forbear, and to be as patient with the refusals as I was pleased with the favours of providence. I found the thought a consoling one, and drank deeply of this sedative of the times and soothing syrup of the seasons, the whiles I remembered that Milton himself was dependent on the turn of the year, and was unable to write, as he once informed a friend of his, from the autumnal equinox to the vernal. For this information I was grateful, as I should never else have had the courage to believe it of myself. Indeed I was not only consoled, I was elated, and felt a pious pride in the blankness of my pages, seeing that the stars in their courses had deigned to fight against me, that the very skies had conspired, and that nothing less than the universe was the cause of it all. I at once lumped Milton into my litanies, sponsored on him all my open spaces, and feeling honoured in humiliation and distinguished in defeat actually went so far as to believe that even nothing attempted was something done. Thus I became more and more enamoured of my idleness, and dawdled and dozed on the endymion eider-down of delay, while the days drifted and the months meandered by, and all my life lapsed into one long lounging lullaby between the grand equinoxes of birth and death.

I have admitted, however, that I wrote trash. I had vowed when writing my diary to be artless, I might almost say innocent, and to my regret found that I was keeping my word. In all forms of literature it is agreeable to be commended for simplicity, but very aggravating to be accused of it, and though many poets have boasted of having lisped in numbers it is perilous to begin lisping in prose. However, I was not discountenanced. I reduced neither myself to despair nor my effusions to the dustbin, but still persevered both in my nothingness and in my next-to-nothingness for a rout of reasons. For instance I realised that though Rome could, by a freak, have been built in a day, a diary by its very nature demanded a number, and I did not doubt that in the course of them I should improve. From hour to hour I should go from strength to strength until in the last triumphs of taste and in the final supremacies of style I should write into every little syllable of time the significance of a library. For this hope I was indebted to no less a writer than Virgil, who, when lapsing into more lowly lingo than was his wont, spoke of wooden props which would serve till the marble columns arrived. So that was the principle, you lumbered first and quarried afterwards, and as lumbering was more in my literary line I lumbered, naturally not with any godless and graceless grudging at heart, but, reflecting that other wise men had also worked in wood, I laboured with abounding solace in the memory of Solomon and the cedars of Lebanon. Everything I wrote was wooden, by design of course, or 'according to plan' as home-bound generals express it, and though as might be supposed I was more prodigal of props and more economic of marble than my master, I was always mindful of the old adage that if you took care of the posts, the columns would take care of themselves. And to this adage I added another, one very sacred in spirit, very apocryphal in form, and very profane in application, namely that the morrow should take thought for the morrow—and incidentally for the marble —enough for the day is the timber thereof.

For years I must have been immured in these mute imaginings, happy to believe that only by nigger-driving the muses, or soundly horsing the heralds of inspiration, should I ever indulge the realised ideal of a diary. I was pleased to think that the chastisement of their peace was upon me, and out of artistic courtesy forbore to retaliate, allowing the dust of idleness and the cobwebs of excuse to settle on the whips and scorpions which might have leathered the Olympian ladies into compliance. But the hour came when I had exhausted all my incense at the silent shrine, when I grew tired of swinging the censer in the one hand and of swinging the lead in the other, and when, having cashed all my courtesy and got very little change out of the deal, I bethought me once more of those whips. And success was mine. I ceased to pray, and began flogging for favours, and the mincing muses who had been speechless in the sanctuary were very eloquent at the cart-tail. And it came about in this way.

One day I not only promised myself a diary but I promised it in public. I published my purpose in the university syllabus, entitled my lectures 'Diary of a journey in England', promised pictures, and on the first day of the vacations set out on my travels. It was like taking fortune at the flood, after drifting in the shallows, flats and backwaters, and finding in every cross wind and cloudy sky a reason for casting anchor till more favourable weather set in. It was like putting my hand to the helm or rather my shoulder to the wheel after idly stretching out my arms in longing for the further shore. It was like shelving the thoughts of the morrow and, for once at least, tackling the deeds of the day. And I did them. Formerly I had been over-nice about my nibs, fastidious about my paper, finicky about my ink, so plausible in my pretenses, so devious and designing in my delays, that I was less stricken in conscience by anything neglected than by anything done. In fact I had become problematic, and could not only think two things at once however contradictory, but worse still, could prove to the satisfaction of all, and at times of my secret self, that both were the same. But my public promise was like a public confession, for whereas confession always closes the door on the past, it is publicity which bolts it. At last I stood exposed, and had no alternative but to honour the vows of reform with the fruits of repentance.

The diary however which I wrote then was not the diary of which I shall speak now, for it was too monotonous. Every lecture which I delivered on my return, no less than every picture which I displayed was a twin brother of the last. Week after week I showed my audience series and series of river scenes, where the difference lay rather in the name of the river than in the character of the scene. In fact England from my lectures appeared to be merely one long river, a mighty meandering Mississippi, flowing on like time without beginning and without end. It was the same a year later when all who attended my lectures left with the idea that England was a conglomeration of race-courses and cathedrals. Every town I entered had a cathedral, and every cathedral town I entered had a racecourse. Indeed it seemed that all England was either praying or racing. The whole land was one piebald panorama of the temple and the turf, an olla podrida of bookmakers and priests, where one hardly knew whether the general hosannas were for the mercies of the Almighty or for the winners of the last chase. And so in the turmoil of my divided pilgrimage to the turf and to the altar, I sometimes sought the bookies and sometimes sought the saints, made my racing card a book-mark for my testament, and said grace and spotted winners with tumultuous abandonment.

It is said that one sees what one will. I think it truer however to say that the eye is never so open as when closed, but the sense is perhaps a little distilled. Looking over my diaries I feel that my eyes have been very faulty servers, though it may be more justly censured that I have not thought as I should nor written as I ought. However that may be, the judgment lies with others, and so to my diary.

CHAPTER TWO

From Bonn to the Hook of Holland

Having decided my tour I packed, and I packed with a skill that in me is born of perfected practice, but which in another could have come only of fasting and prayer. Indeed so perfected is my practice and so practised my perfection, that I never fast and never pray, at least until I unpack, and then my prayers are very fervent, and the pauses between very profane. In packing a man does not mind, and I rejoice in my own gender. There is no pride of place in my bag at all, no aristocracy of articles, no caste distinction between the tooth-brushes and the boots, no bar to communion between the chocolate and my most intimate and inexpressible things of wear. To pack in more than any ten such bags can hold is my accomplishment, and neither trivialities of taste nor superstitions of propriety distress me in the democratic dragonnade of my art. Every hole is suffocated up, every gap grouted out to the neck, every rift rammed and hammered up to the throbbing throat with a welter of what-nots, collars, hairwash, handkerchiefs, sandwiches and socks till finally a grand clog fantastic on the bulging lot levels the last rebellious billows into line. I have one reason and one advantage. With a single bag I am a mobile animal, with baggage I am the Siamese twin of every porter who endeavours to catch my eye. There were days, I admit it, days when I stumbled beneath the blundering abundance of my own impedimenta, when I was a bugbear to passengers and porters alike, a blocker of corridors and of carriage doors, not only a rock of offence when I was waiting for the train but also a breaker of public shins when I was in it, there were days, yes, but those days are done. I have gained if not in conscience, at least in courage since then. Indeed while my friends have been waving from the platform, and while their good-byes have still been echoing in my ears I have taken the oozing jam sandwiches which I had sworn to eat, and the bundles of flowers I had promised to deliver, and shot them out through the window on the other side, without one atom of mercy or of remorse. I have even outpointed the apostle himself, and leaving mountains to be moved by others, have bestowed all my sticks on porters and given my umbrella to be burned in pursuance of the eminently philosophic and practical faith: thou shalt have no other bags but one. For that is the loveliest and most lasting of all alliances, a single man with a single bag, and never was a couple so constant and so without encumbrance, so dead to divorce and so set against all separation, as that one and indivisible Darby and Joan of the road, my simple self and that bag of mine.

But there are dangers. I once knew an Englishman who came to Germany during the days of the inflation, in those tearaway times when millionaires were lamenting their millions, and when everybody was sighing for the unciphered yesterdays when he had less and possessed more. And this young Englishman was one of those who had little and possessed much. He came, he saw, and he cornered. Although very sparing of his pence in England he became very prodigal of his billions abroad, and in this spate of paper prosperity, he purchased, and he bargained, and he bought everything but a pantechnicon to take the things back. But the time for taking them back came, and on the evening of his departure I called round, peeped into his room, and lo there he was, sitting in the shadow of his piled-up booty, and buried in a despair as deep as his possessions were high. He was depressed. I sympathised. Could I help him? I could! One glance at the bags explained all. He was a young man, of the simple sort, void of that devious and designing understanding which has been my proud boast and my still prouder possession in all matters of travel. O the empty simplicity of his packing! I more than smiled. Mine was the loud laugh that spoke the vacant bags! He had packed one with nothing more than a suit and an atmosphere, and in the rest were layers of shirts loosely and lightly welling up in the ample and circumambient air. Now atmosphere is very welcome on the Alps or in art, but not in bags. There is no point in breathing spaces and elbow room, seeing there is nothing to breathe and seeing there are no elbows to move. No, I have a remedy. I just whispered one word into that young Englishman's ear, a word that dissipated the atmosphere from his bags as effectively as it dispersed the depression from his heart. Rolling! ROLLING! Did he understand? Well, did he? We seized those suits, and hanging on either end with the struggling grimness of a tug-of-war we rolled them into the compass and consistency of lead pencils. My word, no slackness there was found! You could have slipped his shirts into a test-tube, you could have threaded a needle with his drawers, you could - with luck and in the dark - have paraded the whole job-lot as a bunch of asparagus, blazers, pyjamas, handkerchiefs and socks, all stretched as tight as a banjo string, and all strangled to the long-drawn-out tenuity of a tapeworm. Nothing was spared the bleeding pressure of our python embrace, and the mighty mass which one brief hour before had seemed to multiply both in mass and might the more we examined it meandered away like macaroni in our cobra-like grasp. I know he was grateful, I am persuaded he mentioned me to monotony in his prayers, I believe - and I have vanity enough to confirm me in my faith - that my photograph and mine alone was in his left breast-pocket all the way from Cologne to Harwich, and then? Gratitude good-bye. His prayers became once more immaculate of all monotony, and that photograph of mine was whisked away from the warmth of his bosom and went - only the winds and waves know whither. It was at the customs. His bags were opened, and as each groaned out its oppressed and pent-up burden, the officials, whose distrust only deepened at the pleading dismay of the poor young man, burrowed in every bag up to the elbows. They did not leave a thing unrolled, and the final vision I have of him is at Liverpool Street Station where he met his very precise father and his mincing martinet of a mother, and where carrying a sheaf of shabby shirts under one arm and a bundle of trailing trousers under the other, with three battered hats on his head, and a madding crowd of pyjamas round his neck he stood looking for all the world like some rakehell American marine-stores on the march or like some broken down old pawnbroker after a rummage sale fired out bag and baggage on to the road.

 Now though this story has its further and more apocryphal phases, how taxi-drivers turned away in disgust, how porters fled in their precipitate pride, and how finally the poor family, having moved the compassion of a costermonger, followed for hours at the distance respectability demands the unhallowed handcart with its jumble of junk, so shamingly and so unmistakably theirs, nevertheless in case I be accused of more fidelity to fiction than to my friend I shall forbear. I had his love once, he shall have my loyalty now, and the veils which courtesy grants, which friendship expects, and which truth demands will now be drawn. Moreover a touch of grief if he only knew it has made us kin again, for, let me admit it, I chance to have a wastrel wardrobe myself, and often wish that reticence were the key to it.

I said that my first note was on packing and I notice that my second is on porters. I well remember why. As I stepped out of the Rheinuferbahn at Cologne I walked into one. He was not of the casual cabby or of the lucky loafer kind, greasy-eyed and hungry-handed, but a really official porter, one with a cap and badge, and furthermore with a bearing that was not to be fobbed off with a few fugitive pfennig and a cigarette. He stepped forward, - I stepped on, - and the peril was past, for it is only a two minute walk from the quay to the station, and as the spires of the great Gothic Cathedral are in sight all the way the distance appears even less. A mark saved is a mark earned, I reflected, and with some pride at this parsimony in myself, and with some pity at the improvidence of my fellows, I strode up the slope by the Hohenzollern Bridge. I had only gone one step, or two steps, or perhaps I had taken three when I felt a touch on my arm and a voice in my ear. Fifty pfennig. It was the first of the freelancers, a big fellow with neither cap nor badge, with a face yellow, city-smoked, and dried, and of course with a bearing that might be blustered into ten pfennig less. I strode on, he strode by my side. Fifty pfennig! And then I left him behind. I was now going up the Frankenwerft, and the Cathedral so rugged in its regularity and so Gothic in its gloom began to grow on my eyes, and once more I was priding myself and pitying my fellows when I was pulled up dead. Twenty pfennig. Right in my path was a somewhat yeasty youth, a tattered and untouchable chap, without a breath of even the pavement respectability of the first freelancer I had met. Twenty pfennig. I had come to Am Dom and had to halt. A tornado of traffic was tearing by, lumbering lorries, tractors, trailers and trams amid such a drift of dust and such a flush of petrol fumes that I almost dropped my bag - and my twenty pfennig - in despair of getting through alone. Twenty pfennig. I wavered and the yeasty youth was at my side, twenty pfennig and he was looking me in the face, twenty pfennig and he was reaching towards my bag, twenty pfennig—and with one spring I was plunging through, in front of this motor, in front of that, doubling round buses, skipping round cars, careering past, through, by and along waggons, vans, charabancs and carts till: Twenty pfennig! - O glory to God, I bumped into the policeman at point and twenty pfennig died away as an echo in my ears. So I had triumphed at last and could lounge onward to the station, could linger along with the loitering and lackadaisical elegance of one who is above the cashy anxieties and pfennig vexations of a wastrel and worried world.

 I had now leisure for other thoughts and had time to look at the Cathedral, which, in its lonely grandeur, seems to stand apart like its own lofty spires aloof from life, stranded as it were away from the common track of men and from the common course of things. It is great art, and yet I felt that with all its greatness Cologne is only a thing of admiration, a pre-eminence admitted, but one that leaves us very much to the distant littleness of ourselves. It is stately but severe, elegant but sombre, and far from allowing us the solace of art and the pleasure of beauty it appears to utter in its grand and gravestone tranquillity the sadness of uncounted confessions and of bitter fullness of prayer. And just as there is nothing of gladness, so there is nothing of kindliness in its grandeur, no humbly-bent benevolence in the far-flung arches and in the vasty vaulting, no familiarity in the high flying spires which apparently brave the blue of space and all but challenge an answer from the voiceless void of the sky. It is as though from scepticism of any responding echo we had made a defiant flourish of our frailty, had indulged in a triumph of our own unnoted tears, and, more in bravado than belief, had persuaded ourselves to an aery height of hope out of the deeps of despair. Such mightiness is the measure of the heart's need and not the meeting of its desires, and one turns away with the thought that communion with the skies is the first as well as the last unhappy vanity of mankind.

I was just about to enter the station when I stumbled across a mere mite of a child. He was a simple masterpiece of mire and misery, a little tearful atom whose tiny dirty hand was already on my bag. Ten pfennig sir! and as I went in he rushed up alongside with me. Do you want the booking office? there it is! and as he ran along he pointed to what no one with eyes could fail to see, the long array of windows and the waiting queues of people. Yes the booking office! There it was! He would mind my bag! Ah! only ten pfennig! And I went to take my stand in the queue naturally with him at my side. I was an Englishman? Yes? Did I want to change my money? There was the place! Just over there! He would take me, - ah, only ten pfennig!—and so he rambled on with his little fingers fast on to mine. There was no help for it, and as I moved up to buy my ticket, I had to drop my bag. He was on it at once - ah thanks, only ten pfennig - and frantically floundering about with my bag he struggled out of the crowd. I could not have been more than a minute, and when after taking my ticket I struggled out of the crowd myself I looked round for him. I found him waiting - and my bag? - gone! But - ! I asked. 'Oh it's all right,' he said simply, 'I have found a porter for you, sir!' and taking me by the arm he pointed to one - the blotch of Egypt on him - my friend of the Rheinuferbahn. Yes, my friend of the Rheinuferbahn, and no other, who with my bag on his shoulder was waiting for the word. I stood as though stricken by the staggers, but porter and professional as he was he did not appear in the least disturbed. He countered my confusion with astute courtesy and studied calm. 'The Hook of Holland? Yes?' he said quietly, 'Platform 4, 5.35, I shall see you there!' Just one touch of his cap, and in the same instant he was carrying off my bag to the train. I did not utter a word. I stupidly stood there, dumb and defeated and done. And my ten pfennig? Well for the sake of his childish blue eyes I gave him ten - and perhaps more - and when on entering the train I bade good-bye to my friend of the Rheinuferbahn - and to my mark - I began to reflect on the ways of mice and men, on the ways of mysterious mice and of mysterious men, and on the ways of myself, most mysterious of all.

Once more I was travelling to England, not via Belgium but via Holland, and this for two reasons, - because of Holland, and because of Belgium. Perhaps I am prejudiced, perhaps too much at the mercy of my many moods, but I am under vow never to cross Belgium again. It is not that I have rakehell recollections nor even heroic ones of the war, not that I am still sore about harrowed hopes, bludgeoned ambitions, and skull-dragged ideals, for the war after all was only something big, something that was neither a climax nor a crash, something that had neither the dignity of drama nor the refreshment of a farce, something that might best be described as a blind political brawl round the public house of high finance. The war was a genuine child of this very ungenuine age, of this age of stunts and stampedes, of this age of the little man and of the big pocket. No, it is not the war that has biased me against Belgium. It is a peddling prejudice which, in a shallow assurance of being just, has sought for proof and found it. It began years ago when I was once travelling to England, and when after a midnight ordeal of impossible passengers, crowded carriages, and yawning waits on the way, I arrived wretched and nerve-racked, with dusty boots, black hands, and a beard, in low and unlovely Ostend, which is in my opinion the classic slum of the West. Ostend never looked so low and so unlovely as then, and as I trudged in the drizzle along the slippery pier I fell foul of the porters. With them my prejudice began. O the porters of Belgium! above all the porters of Ostend Pier! Bustling, bellowing, perspiring footpads, fellows whose life is one long campaign for pence, one gasping steeplechase after the centimes! fellows who do not earn, fellows who pilfer their pay, who, turning your open hand into an empty one, charge extra on generosity and jump the change. It was these men, the denizens of the very dredge-beds of Ostend, who hardened my first and trifling aversion into a dour dislike, for being neither sailors nor landsmen they belong to that mongrel element, which, having never coursed the deeps, knows only the depths when ashore.

Yes, it is otherwise in Holland, and also whenever I leave for England, I long for the evening peeps over the

North German Plain. I saw it once in darker and more distressful days, and associations as lasting as life itself brood over it now in my eyes. I lent it my sadness then, and as I looked out into the lowering half-lights of the evening it seemed that the dim deeps of the fading horizon indulged my despair. It may be my own famished fancy, a craving for echoes that never come, but I still lose myself in the solemn and insinuating stillness of the North German Plain, in its long, quiet, contemplative stretches of farm and field, in its touches of wistful woodland, in its calm and grey religious skies. There is an air of our dreaming idyllic East Anglia about it, the same glimpses of quaint windmills, of old barns, of seemingly lost and lonely spires, and now and then of distant endymion villages which appear to lie beyond all sound of the wakening world. Such scenes as these favour a feeling for the eternal quietudes, and in their wide views, spacious landscape, and full plentitude of cloud and sky, open up the boundless beyond, and suffuse us with a sense of those things we only feel yet never know.

 I have no other impressions of these parts but from the railway carriage window, a spot which would seem the least suited of any to muse on the all but permanent and prairie peace of the Northern Plain. Yet casual and scattered as my glimpses were, broken into by the bustle of others and interrupted by talk, they left me with a pleasing emphasis of the silence in the woods and the fields. As night drew on there came an accent of calm into the landscape, unuttered tones of stillness, a breath of that lightly breathing ease that lives in dreams of the clay and knows no time. Deep in the untroubled drift of the evening, in the lingering lights and delaying dimness of earth and sky, I felt a pause, a tarrying as it were of the eternities, a suspense as moving and as motionless as the poise of a far-off bird in the breeze. Perhaps there is a vanity in thoughts such as these, when we make of our own moods a mood of nature, yet in this vanity all faith and belief is first experienced and finally preserved, and buoyed up as we may be by preciser opinions and by exacter science, we are no nearer knowledge than in those devotional days when the world was still wide and the seas unsounded, when the hills were everlasting, and when no one knew the whence and whither of the wind.

But to return to the train. I have often wondered when exiled to the corridor, tired by the stale and stalemated talk of my fellow travellers, whether an old hope of mine will ever be fulfilled. It is a very old hope, one of those hopeless hopes which I indulge the more since I know it to be vain, of meeting someone by chance who would leave more memory on my mind than that he was gone. During my travels I have been tumbled into many intimacies, but no one has ever entered with sure and steady tread into mine. It is not that my patience has failed. I have with the utmost valour fumbled on all fours with the fag-end philosophy of the travelling public: I have waded waist deep in the wash-out wisdom of the world of everyday. I have talked vapour with the best, the vain and profane vapour of the weather and of where I have been, and I have trailed away interminable stretches of time in the trivialities of railway routine, of sport, and of the news. But in vain. My memory of all those I have met, and of all they have said, has no more enduring detail than the smudge and the scream of those flying expresses which hurtled the other way past our own. Personality is rare. Our civilisation, appealing as it does more to the senses than to the mind, has spoiled us for thought. Our eyes are held up by the headline, our ears are dunned and deafened by advertisement. The mind of to-day is not a delicate adjustment of ideas, a fine and precise balance for the weighing of whys and wherefores. The mind of today is a mediocre marine-stores where the most futile of information is shot in like coal from a cart. It cannot help itself. It can close no windows, it can shut no doors. The siren of sensation is able to scream through the thickest walls. In the newspapers, in the clubs, in the railway carriage, at home and out of it - Gene Tunney, Gene Tunney, is getting married, is getting married, Charlie Chaplin, Charlie Chaplin, has got a divorce, has got a divorce, Bernard Shaw has written a play, a play, a play. Have you read it? Have you read it? This is very sorry fodder for the soul. We have a science of diet, there is a movement known as food-reform, we are very careful of our kitchens, we study our tables with very narrowed eyes. But no one has ever bestowed a tithe of this care to a diet of the mind. No, the modern mind is a universal waste-paper basket. It is a public dust-bin, without the blessing of a bottom and without the saving grace of a handle. It is a farrago of facts not a discipline of ideas. It is a gazetteer gone wrong, it is a dictionary of explanations without the words.

Still as I stood in the corridor from Nijmegen to Rotterdam, aided as much by the darkness without as by the drowsiness within, I came to more amiable and even to more majestic emotions. Very everyday though my fellow travellers might be, and very unsuspecting in their piracy of spurious opinion, though they were at best well-thumbed anthologies of other men's thoughts, and at worst scrappily garbled and Quarto Editions of the *Sketch* and of the *Mail*, still they gathered distinction in a reflection which I read years ago in *Les Mémoires d'outre Tombe*. We are all children of the shadow, and when we meet it is only as mere motes in the immeasurable unknown. For the most part we touch each other but once in Life's passage, and then, letting our mutual memories die away in the echo of our good-byes, we pass on for ever. This is the thought of Chateaubriand in those *Mémoires d'outre Tombe*, a thought that is written with a more solemn setting and with a finer flourish of feeling in the grand regality of his panoramic prose. He had left France for America, and in the long loneliness of the Atlantic voyage they chanced one day on another vessel eastward bound. It was towards the fall of the evening and an air of prayerful peace was slumbering on in the dying dazzle of the day. They approached, slackened sail, and halted awhile, and then after some simple syllables of greeting they bade each other god-speed and good-bye. Once more they let out sail, and as the stranger slowly swayed away over the waves to the east, all crowded on the stern and all waved their everlasting farewells. For an hour they strained after her till at last she was just a sinking silhouette in the eastern sky. One shimmer on the horizon and she was gone, and with her had gone their last sight of all those on board, men who, having once parted, would become more and more dispersed and finally lost as the raindrops in the seas. Farewell! Godspeed! Yet, as Chateaubriand concludes, sail to what ports they will, eternity is the final haven of them all.

I might have sauntered on through these stately thoughts of over a century ago, and in spirit have drifted even farther than the farthest west, but for a too obvious English lady, a very masculine, very modern, and moreover a very middle-aged emergency, whose manners like her hair and skirt were in very reduced circumstances. I have never savoured the society of these lemon-faced and petticoated acid-drops, whose talk is all of equality - a dubious ideal accessible only in the law-courts - and who tirade against tyranny and trousers by usurping both and by gracing neither. They have also what is very fashionable to-day: a cut and staccato tone, a pert abruptness of speech, supposed - by those who are fools to suppose it - to indicate decision of character and masterliness of mind. My too obvious English lady, who happily was more obvious than English, though more obviously anything, but alas, - a lady, had this mannerism, which, added as I divined to the other distinguished trophies of the sexual war, cocktails and cigarettes, proclaimed the liberty and equality of the modern woman, whose fraternity however I beg to be spared. Naturally it is not from the personality of modern women that I shrink, but from the ape-like portrait of something better, the rakish resemblance which lowers our illusion of what is best, and daubs our dreams with the common dirt of the day. Maybe I am too delicate in my ideals, of too fine and refined a scruple in questions of sex, and shrink more from a caricature of what is good, more from innocence that has been sullied and for ever spoiled, more from purity that has been polluted and from beauty that has been profaned than from the blackest unbettered badness and unblushable shame. For me the tears of things lie less in what is than in what might have been, less in the rude realities than in the regretful recollections of those uncashed and uncashable graces of life, graces which perhaps even gain in grace when so lightly thrown away.

It was thus that when facing my too obvious English lady I was afraid. She was a most modern woman, or rather a meagre masquerade of a man, being only a woman because certified so at birth, and only in that sense a man, in which she, so abusive of men, was pleased to conceive them. She began to appeal to me on all doubtful points, to plunge me into personal embarrassments, and to corner me with all kinds of enquiries of how, and why, and who. I am merely a man, meek and accommodating, but I vowed inwardly to be a victim neither of excessive courtesy on my part, nor of cow-eyed curiosity on hers. Even my acquaintance at home never goes beyond the complimental. Confidences would alarm us both, and confessions would argue either a lapse of grace on their part or a collapse of common-sense on my own. So at first I tried to subdue her with some very dubious German, and was gravelled by her replies which were couched in more dubious German still. There was no escape along the corridor which she blocked or back into the compartment which she would again be tempted to enter. Perhaps I prayed, perhaps some sympathising angel saw my surging sorrows of soul, perhaps the legions in the limbo lent their supplications to reinforce mine - I shall never know. Really against gooseflesh in all senses I am no hero, but help was at hand. The dinner steward came round and she took a ticket, but in a panic lest I should receive the next ticket in sequence I drew the steward aside and whispered to him my appeal. 'Give me a ticket that puts a whole carriage between me and that woman there!' He looked me quizzically up and down, and then mistaking my intention, took a sly peep into the next compartment. He thought I was seeking fairer game. I gave him a most negative nod. He returned it with an equally negative smile, and winking gave me the bottom ticket of all. Thus it was that I dined in peace, but so precarious was my possession of the poor peace which I had obtained that I never left the car till I arrived at the Hook of Holland.

CHAPTER THREE

To Ely, with thoughts on Ely Cathedral

I notice that my diary is blank about the passage from the Hook of Holland to Harwich, and will ever remain so. Whatever may have happened, whether it was still or stormy on the way, whether I slept or lay awake, whether I beguiled the time either in platitudes with the other passengers or in tussles with the stewards, all memory of the voyage has passed away from my mind as tracklessly as drifting clouds from the sky. I have one recollection, and moreover I made a note at the time about the customs. There are some travellers who perhaps through fear of missing the train or with the ambition of a better seat in it lie awake all night, and begin to enquire in the very minor hours of the morning whether we have arrived. In the flutters of their fear they get up to make certain, they are washed and shaved at two, fully dressed at half-past, and after many anxious exits and just as many non-plussed returns they venture to the upper deck to welcome the first rays of the rising moon at three. Having in the meantime confided their anxieties to the captain, inquisitioned the crew, stampeded all the unfortunate stewards on duty, bombarded the breakfast room with corkscrew enquiries as to the activities of the cook, they return to their cabins with the reassuring news that we shall be hours yet, after which the exits and the entrances are renewed, and the great investigation as to when we shall arrive once more set on foot. It is here where my notes and my recollections begin. My diary for the day opens up with the words patience and philosophy, not written in irony of others but as a tribute to myself, a tribute which though paid but once is a memory I shall always preserve. I have reason to thank God that I am not as others are, for I have never dunned a steward before his own patronising time, I have never cumbered the gangway with my bag, barracked porters along the quay, blockaded the barriers, elbowed the officials, or stormed the trains. Though cool and elegantly last when leaving the boat I have always contrived to be, if not first, in the very first and unfluttered line of those who have leisure to choose their seats in the waiting express. And for a reason. The passport office obliterates all priority, and then the customs like death is a very great leveller. Perhaps I have that disarming and diplomatic honesty of eye and heart, that assumed and unassuming simplicity that surpasses all official understanding, but I enter the customs as I enter a London lift. I come, and keep on going. There are two simple and open-Sesame secrets of my unfailing success, apart from the patience and philosophy, the influence of which is perhaps more felt than observed. The first is to open the bags without being asked, however small the bags may be and however incriminating the contents. And the second secret is, when shown a list of the dutiable goods, to take the list, to note all the items, and at the same time to utter a heart-felt and considered 'no' to each in turn. There will be no examination, and in less than five minutes you are choosing a corner seat.

Now I had always desired to see East Anglia from the first time that I had heard the name, and I could never hear it afterwards without feeling some of the solitude in which history has left it, and without in fancy lending it those demurer delights which I had dreamed of when crossing the North German Plain. I had visions of East Anglia, and I let my fantasy play with the ancient syllables, and fashion them into a fable of things that once were, when the Conqueror was still conquering and when Hereward the Wake was still defiantly haunting the woods and fens. Nor when history had spent its inspiration was my own idealism idle, and with every mention of those ever-mentionable names, Ipswich, Norwich, Cambridge, and Ely, I would be gazing over broad acres of Arcadian grace, and would be pleasuring in prospects of pure pastoral beauty which even the raw and rugged reality has wholly failed to dispel. This idealism came I think of seeing Ely, not on a visit, but from the carriage window when I was once on my way abroad. It was just a glimpse, a casual glance which I littered at the time amid the listless lumber of so many other travelled memories, but which I was always pleased to recall in my lonely and more leisureable hours. We had halted at Ely, and in the late light of the afternoon I was only half aware of the Cathedral, which, lost in outline and sombred in enveloping shadows, seemed to gather in itself the uncanny grandeurs of the darkening sky, and to take on a spectral character in gloomy keeping with the sedate associations of religion and age. Of the town I had no rigid recollection, only an obscure and umbered impression of the Cathedral, an outstanding sense of something which was distantly and divinely sundered from all that I had seen during the day. I thought at the time, in one of those flights of fabling fancy to which I am over prone, that if ever I turned recluse, if ever I were to flee the face of the world and were to lose myself in some nameless and unknown anywhere it would be in Ely. Alas, an expansive bosom is often the seat of a puffed and hollow heart. But I anticipate. With such thoughts as these I bought a ticket for Ely. In my compartment were two others, a young lady and a gentleman, whom I recognised from their language to be Swiss. I know no speech which is ugly, for even those which grate on the unstudied ear have their distinctive tones and relative rhythms, and have, when spoken well, their fulness and fascinating ascents and falls of sound. But there is none that I have ever heard which has such a myriad music, such a chromatic compass of the whole singing scale, such lingering lilts, such melting modulations, as some of the dying dialects of Swiss German. There are touches of it in Italian, traces in Anglo-Irish of which the legato undulations of the Last Rose of Summer are perhaps a reminiscence, but they never hover so in their own harmonies, nor glide in the delicately graded octaves of those Swiss dialects to which I refer. Used as I am to the steady staccato tread of High German, and - in comparison of course - to its uncouth and kettledrum character, I have a redoubled longing for the speech melody of the South, for its peculiar prettiness of pitch, its chorded accent, and for its tuneful turns of tone. To hear this is for me an event, and so I determined to slip Ely, and to stay in the train till Liverpool, for as I gathered from the talk of my fellow passengers they were bound for Canada and would be sailing by the C.P.O. the same afternoon. I was well settled in this decision when the young lady turned round and addressed me in an outburst of beggarly and bedraggled English. I do not know whether I replied, or whether in my confusion my lips trembled out something that was mistaken as such, but for a sinking second or two I groped and gazed like the old monk of the story shake out of centuries of sleep. And then that girl talked-in torrents. I know I cast one drowning glance at her companion, struggled for a time with some straws of German, but borne along the Niagara Rapids of that girl's gush I was unable to turn the tide. For two floundering hours I was buffeted by her linguistic waves and wind, swept over foaming falls of froth, swilled along a babbling St. Lawrence away into a broad Atlantic Ocean of illimitably small beer. I should have been overwhelmed even had the girl been English, but as she was a foreigner, cracked in accent and girded with the grossest ungrammar of the Far West, I left the train at Ely as lacerated as the language of my native land.

As I stood on the station platform I bade the prate-pump a benediction of good-byes, sang inwardly a Solomon's song in laudation of Ely, and then - in both senses - very spiritually bent in the knee I thanked God for my deliverance from the treadmill of that woman's tongue. I have not lost my love of Swiss German, but I have reflected since that one thoughtful advantage of being in some places abroad is that I do not understand anything that is said. The mystery of a language wholly foreign is compensation for its emptiness, banalities have all the refreshment of riddles, and wind the weight of wisdom. I can consort with the most commonplace acquaintance and remain uncritical, I can confide in the hollowest of friends with profit. Indeed so magnified is my modesty in a land to the speech of which I am an entire stranger, that I find myself doffing my hat to the dullest, only too pleased to be the pupil of any peasant, and at times even happy when in the confidence of the coarsest guttersnipe, ready to be levelled to the lowest in my love of learning and glad - in the chastening thought of the Scriptures - when a little child shall lead me. I still marvel at the speech music of the gorges of Graubünden, and live again, in the echoes of its lyric loveliness, those thoughts which perhaps after all were only my own. For there is wealth in illusion, cash in accounts on which we never draw, and always credit where there is no question of its being claimed, so that when my Swiss illusions steamed away from Ely I felt all the poorer, not for being poor, but for knowing it.

I strolled out of the station, and then stood for a minute in dazed indecision on the road outside. Had I not seen the Cathedral and assured myself it was Ely before I alighted I should have returned to enquire. As it was I stood stock-still in the road, wondering not only why I was there but whether I really wanted to continue my way into the town. Somehow I felt that the whole world was aware of my hesitation and I thought of covering up my confusion by turning to the time-tables and noting the departure of the trains, or by looking up the porter and plying him with questions to which my own sense could furnish an answer. The station, however, looked very deserted now, as though the last flutter of life had been draughted out of it, train, passengers, porter, and the odd staring stray idler gone, and away round the corner I could see the last hotel bus lumbering along empty into the town. A moment more and it had gone as well, leaving the world to darkness and to me and to the debris of many dreams.

So this was Ely! and I who had in fancy been communing in the chaste asceticism of the Cathedral close, or moving along the avenued approach of spacious beech trees, ancestral elms, and stately cedars, saw nothing else ahead of me but a very beery and unbeatific public house, which, like a sort of sodden end of a Saturday afternoon, appeared to be propped up amid other dwellings as dubious and unsabbatarian as the pub itself. Moreover, lurching past them were some very weekday and very wastrel fellows, not walking nor even strolling, but drifting about like a forlorn overflow from the East End. I shall never know why I did not stay where I was standing. I did not decide to go. I had not even the resolution to reflect about my return, but somehow or other I found myself slumming it through Ely, looking neither to the right nor to the left, but having the impression of a litter of low-browed houses which hovelled on either side of the road. I remember passing the park gate and being too embarrassed to peep in. I remember hurrying past the west door of the Cathedral without a glance, as though I were ashamed to be thought as coming for that alone, or as though I were some poor bridegroom who valiantly affects to see neither the fuss nor the presents and begins to consider everything else with a very strenuous unconcern. I studied shop windows as if in a despairing search of something I wanted to buy, examined the street signs with the air of one who is lost but who is determined to be found, and I bought a paper and scanned it with such eager exactness as almost to persuade myself that I desired to read it. How often I consulted my watch for the time which I already knew, went through my pocket book for cards which I never expected to discover, and dotted unnoticeable dots in my diary I shall never know. But when I had sorted and re-sorted the last of my tattered letters, adjusted my glasses, and sharpened every pencil that I had, I observed a photographer's shop on the far side of the road and my courage returned. Apparently it was no cynicism to carry a camera in those parts, and reflecting that Ely though low to a critical eye might be merely lowly to a kindly one I crossed over.

Now there was little to be seen in the window display of that photographer's shop. In fact there was nothing else but a spread of poorly parochial portraits, weedy wedding parties, children for confirmation, father in his Sunday penitentials, and the like, most of them with very upholstered expressions and in over-obvious and plebeian poses, and all of them without exception upcountry examples of the mere many of Ely. But one card caught my eye. It was of a young girl placarded over with appeals for the growing of sugar beet in Cambridge. Just a fancy-dress figure, admitted, but excellent as copy for my lectures, and, as illustrating the campaign against German sugar, of double interest to my students. I entered at once with a view to buying it but was told by the lackadaisical girl behind the counter that it was not for sale. I explained, but all my persuasions thudded up against her dullness in vain. I pressed to see the proprietor, and after many ins and outs, further whatfors, series of I-sees, dallying and dunderheading, the girl gave me the picture at last. 'We do not do it as a rule,' she said for the thousandth time, and then glancing at the card continued, 'but, we understand, she is a very nice girl!' I never blush, but had I remained another second my face would have made faggots of the shop.

Then I went to the Cathedral for my shame was gone. I should enter that west door, I resolved, shut my eyes to the shadows and look only to the light of things. I should go in, as I saw others go in, suffused with sanctity and satisfaction, draw in my bated and bewildered breath at first sight of the nave, sigh my way through the aisles, and sink in a seraphic and stricken contemplation of the choir. I should, with an affected familiarity and an open Baedeker, muse on each monument in turn. I should scrutinise the inscriptions, and ponder over the tombs, even though the names were as unknown as the persons who bore them and once noted, never more remembered. And then after my American-tripper round I should write as everyone else would write that the nave was noble, the choir exquisite, and the lady chapel among the most charming in England. There would perhaps be a further note that the general impression was superb, but that the dinner afterwards might have been better and the price less. And so I entered.

However trifling I might have been on entering the door, my lightness went as it closed behind me, for never have I seen anything of such subduing sadness as the Norman nave of Ely Church. Even in the most sombre sights of distress and death in the world outside, there is still the wakening light of day, still some touch of a living hand, some vibration of other yet fellow voices, some soul-alleviating something that bears a brighter promise to the broken spirit, and reveals amid the gloom and clouds a glimpse of the clear sky. But these overwhelming walls of Ely Cathedral seemed to have closed on the light of life for ever, and as I stood in the dimness and dankness of that vast vault I felt the full terror of the thought, that the feet which had first walked there, that the voices which had first echoed there, that the eyes which had set those heavy arches and had looked with gladness towards the growing grace of the choir were dead for evermore. I had stepped into a lofty sepulchre of stone, a mausoleum of mediaeval memory, one of the stately desolations of Isaiah which served as proof of the failing frailty of humanity, and as a wrecking rebuke to perspiring ambition and pride. In the distance was just one glimmer, that of the choir, but between, from the far gates to the door behind me, all was swept bare. All was empty, dark, and still. Not a breath, not a footfall! Nothing to move the emotion, nothing to dispel the deadening dread of death, but all shrouded in shadow, grey as a forgotten grave, built up and barricaded above like a tomb, and all below, in the sombre seclusion of the aisles, the hard flags of unremembered burials, tablets to long-since nameless names, mural memorials to the well-noted unknowns of past time. Never have my thoughts been so reduced to the downtrodden dust of human destiny and of human despair as in the nave and in the aisles of Ely Church.

Weighed down by sentiments such as these I had not observed that I had come to the central space, when, as it were in the turn of an instant, the whole light of the superlative lantern broke upon me. I was standing under the great octagonal dome, an architecture of such genial elegance and grandeur, that he who has seen it and not thought there is a touch of divinity in us, a lingering grace of the skies that gives us some hope of a greater grace to come, must be as one without music. I am a pure pagan, but as I beheld the work of our own Alan of Walsingham I was prepared to believe in inspiration, to believe in a benevolent breathing from the beyond, and in courteous communications from some superior spirit who takes our favoured ones by the hand, and who leads them with a studied certainty of step to the sure summits of art. Here also as in the nave was an air of Isaiah, but not an air of humiliated hope and of toppled ambition, not an air of that grovelling decree—from ashes to ashes, from dust to dust—but a piece of that poetical splendour where the children of the valleys, sitting in darkness and sorrow perceive the first peep of the sun over the hills, the feet of Him who brings the good tidings, the assurance that, despite all the marches of misery and the ravages of evil, the God of Zion still reigns. Here also was a breaking forth into joy, a singing together, as though the very stones of the building had broken forth from the death-grip of those sepulchral aisles and had raced up into the geometric rills and traceried rhythms of the dome itself, and assembling into one choiring whole of interlacing lights and lines were triumphing in the delicate intricacy of their skill. But through all these variegated involutions of voice, through all this ordered and inordinate dithyramb of design, there was the redeeming and dominating tone that promises the defeat of death and the breaking of the tomb, the splitting of the everlastingly-long and soul-stifling silence of the skies, the enduing of the dust with life once more, and the intimacies of eternity. For there are after all echoes across the centuries, whisperings through space and time, revelations one to another even from beyond the grave, as this from our own forgotten Alan of Walsingham whose spirit is still to be seen by those who choose to see it, and whose vanished voice still reverberates in that dome which is as unique as the neglect of him who made it.

It is one step into the choir, but it is a step into the eternities, a step out of the turmoil of every day into the settled assurance of those thoughts which bring peace at birth and which minister tranquillity at the grave. I have seen more grandiose, buildings, buildings that exact awe and that demand admiration, but I have seen none of such unfailing fascination as the choir at Ely. It does not lie merely in the living lightness of line and in the grace of the plurally-pillared columns, superlatively light and graceful as both are, not merely in the fine fluting of the arches and in the studious delicacy of the detail, nor indeed in any of the outer accidents of art. Above the excelling elegance of style there is something which one recollection of Cologne helped to reveal. Cologne is grand but too grand, a labour which dares the admiration of the beholder, and which in its triumph of conscious grace and of deliberate beauty is more a thing of architecture than a cathedral. How many times have I entered it and then halted half irresolute near the great door? And how many times have I, quite by instinct, turned my back on the altar and strained my eyes up those mighty piers which soared away into the obscurity of the vaulted roof? And how many times have I walked along those gloomily Gothic aisles, wandering like a mote in immensity, shadowed down into a dot with no space for any emotions but those of astonishment and of being alone? But astonishment is a painful pleasure, and loneliness is a poor feeling in a house of prayer. Unlike Cologne however, Ely is more than a building, it is a Cathedral. It is great, but within the understanding of men, majestic without magnificence, dignified without aloofness, grand without loss of grace. Its curves bend elegantly down, but calmly, kindly, benignantly, as though intent on hearing the lowly hopes of those in despair below. Indeed in the unassuming splendour of its lovely aisles, and in the mild illumination of the gently lanceted East window, the most despondent will not fail to come to more pleasing persuasions, the most sceptic to feel response to unspoken prayer, the most lonely to be stilled in those longings which slowly lacerate the heart. For the harmony of Ely choir is of the humility of man and of the exaltation of God, the union of the aspiring and of the stooping spirit, that historic covenant of grace, the seal of which is silence, and the signature - the signature of all things.

CHAPTER FOUR

Peterborough, and other Matters

A day later I was in Peterborough and in my diary there is nothing but a note of the fact. It is not that I saw less, nor were my impressions less permanent, but owing to one of the trifling off-chances of time and tide I failed to enter into the intimacies of things as at Ely. For Ely Cathedral afforded more than the pleasures of impression and the benefits of experience, it offered a revelation, an open revelation of religion with its deep array of reminiscence, solemn sanction of time, and with its all but universal yes of mankind. From the art of Alan of Walsingham I learned to sever those feelings which are the heartful heritage of humanity from their peculiar expression, and to see in this peculiarity, whether atheist, Christian, Mahometan, Buddhist, or Jew, something as shallow and as interchangeable as the surface of the sea. I learned that a difference in idiom or a divergency in dialect involves little or none in thought, and that however alien the language of others may be they utter nothing that we never utter ourselves.

Before entering Ely I was very sceptical of ecclesiastic-ism, and, if possible, still more so of Cathedrals, as I thought they partook of the spectacular, and therefore savoured of untruth. Moreover I was most sceptical of the Anglican Communion itself. If asked why, I should perhaps trace my dislike to reading when a boy an article by Emerson, who indulged in some genialities on the Church. He appeared to regard it as a spiritual Hague Convention, and I came to think of it myself as a sort of well-meaning armistice between God and the Devil, a pacifist frame-up between the salvation scufflers of nonconformity on the one hand, and the more beatific bantam-cocks of the Catholic Church on the other. Moreover I learned from Emerson that the hierarchy was aristocratic, and that being a close social preserve and a Pandora's box of the politician, it was raffled among those younger sons who were homeless at home, and all abroad elsewhere. Its creed, according to the same authority, was pre-eminently one of good breeding, its catechism a breviary of good taste. Indeed the only saving grace in the eyes of the Church was the grace to be saved.

Now such thoughts as these I treasured up and made my own, not because they were true, but because, if hostility to the Church was to mean anything at all, they ought to be. I had some return of these sentiments, I admit, when taking my last look of Peterborough Church. It was in the deepening dusk of the late afternoon, and as I looked at the Cathedral from beyond the park it appeared so forbiddingly large and so gloomily old against the ragged clouds of the evening that I turned involuntarily away. Later on as I sat by the cosy bright light of the inn fire I thought of it again. I asked the maid who had just come in if she knew where I could find the dean, as I should like to take a picture of the choir next day. She knew nothing of the dean, nothing of the Cathedral. She had never been in the Cathedral. 'Never?' I asked. 'Never!' She always went to St. John's, but the Cathedral —no!—never! and she looked as blank as though I had addressed her in Hebrew.

But perhaps the maid was over-simple, which was not surprising, seeing that the landlord also was one of very insinuating innocence and of such simplicity as to deceive, not the elect, but himself. I was still sitting by the fire, trying to dream away the blanks in my diary, when he came in, and after some words on the weather he remarked that should I require the stock room it was at my disposal, and that were I in need of anyone in the morning to carry my samples there was a man at the house. At first I thought that in the flitting light of the fire he had mistaken me for another, for there is no one who has less finance in his features than I have, no one who so wears the air of looking at life in the light of leisurely yesterdays as myself. I bent low over the fire to let the gleams play on my face, and even moved my chair out of the shadow to help my host to other views. I have never been thought a commercial before, and years ago I should have felt a grievance, though with the materialism of advancing age I am more mellow towards merchants than I was. I even number one among my friends, naturally not for his business ability, but for the good conscience with which he forgets the cares of cash when once he has closed the office door. To be considered a commercial therefore argued a misdemeanour somewhere, but though I poked the coal, raked the ash, and provoked the blazes to very brilliant purpose, my host was not to be enlightened. I suppose he thought it all to be a friendly advance of which he took advantage, for he approached the fire, and later sat down and talked for a good hour. Before he left he reminded me once more of the stock-room, and dropped one further hint about my samples and the man.

So I had achieved it at last! Well I remember in tighter days, when even the halfpence had a dignity of their own, when the thought of a hotel made my heart beat and the prospect of a bill broke it, how I envied those who, with their shop-talk and seemingly shop-lifting ideas, could bounce the proprietor for reduced terms. Reduction for commercials was, I think, the most rankling of all my thoughts, and though I had often flattered myself that I could sit down unwashed and undetected among the publicans and sinners, that I could croak with the crows, and could jingle the small change of commercial-room chatter to the delusion of the landlord and of all the house, I have imposed on no one, and after the pursiest impersonations have paid my civil score like the rest. I have known men enter hotels in a haste as real as it was assumed, men who have dunned for every item from the telephone and the directory to a taxi and a dinner, men who have businessed it from booking a room to paying for it next day, and spent every hour between trading over the table, bartering with the bread and butter, and commercialising in their cups, men who after supper hauled forth their love-letters and mused over them with the mercantile intensity of cracksmen about to wreck the American ring, and next morning I have seen these superlative bluffers, these Garricks and Kembles of the counting house, being served with the bills of normal folk. I even knew a man who, under the pretence of not wishing to forfeit his seat by the fire, called for a sheaf of envelopes, and for want of a table addressed them on his knee to fictitious firms throwing each on to the floor at his feet, and I saw the landlord wink to the boots to stamp every one, there must have been thirty at least, and then left him with the embarrassment in the morning. I know other cases, cases which happened long ago, and which in the space of years have perhaps been bounteously over-baptised in the rosewater of my unmanageable imagination, and so I shall refrain. Romance is apt to run riot at times in relations of mine, and therefore I shall conclude where in truth I began by saying that here I was in Peterborough without pose and without pretence regarded as a commercial gentleman, and with every prospect of the special favour which attends this consideration.

This was among my first experiences of an English inn, and I suppose an English inn is the crossroad where tradition and truth are more undivinely divided than at any other. There was a time, and it is scarcely two hundred years ago, when Shenstone could scratch on the window of the Red Lion that life elsewhere was a dull round, and that the warmest welcome which ever awaited him was at an inn. Shenstone was, maybe, a man with very desolate ideals, whose life was one long sigh for a happiness which he could never hope to attain. His praise is less a lyric on inns, than an elegy on his own farewell hopes of shepherdess society and of the crook of contentment. But I do not wish to impugn the perfections of the Red Lion, of which Johnson himself had recollections when he remarked to a company, in which there were no dissentient voices, that the highest of human felicities was a corner seat at a tavern fire. And is not the most panoramic of our poetry, I speak of the Prologue to the Canterbury Tales, about the untouchable Tabard Inn of Southwark, and about the all-excelling landlord who led the compay of his guests, so coarsely grave and so cavalierly gay, to the shrine of Thomas-a-Becket? Who has not rejoiced in this, the most illustrious of all inn scenes, in this symphony of the cloister and the gutter, in this unrivalled rhythm of riff-raff and religion, in this choice and cheering rough-and-tumble in the Abraham's bosom of the pubs of long ago? I rejoiced in these things once, read them, and admired. But who, however flushed with fancy could, in a modern inn, thwack up even the thinner enthusiasms of Washington Irving, who, in the loneliness of the Red Horse at Stratford, praised the poker as the sceptre of his domestic empire, and who deemed himself, in the undisturbed dominion of his armchair, a monarch of the inner intimacies of the home? For my part, I felt at Peterborough, despite the special favour of a reduction for commercials, more like the shorn lamb of Sterne, which went astray on an unsentimental journey, and which, though abandoned to the untempered breezes, was only too glad to escape from the crook next day.

Good hotels in England are dear, and bad hotels still dearer. I do not pretend to an ample purse, but I have a free one, and I am prepared for the worst when I receive the best in return. But almost the only best that I have received was abroad. There are two menus in England, one spuriously French and usuriously expensive, and the other is the unending daily dilemma of roast beef and Yorkshire pudding, or roast mutton and mint sauce. And I might say that I never cut either in any hotel in the land, without feeling that I have landed on the hard horn of the dilemma itself, and without sighing for a blasting charge, which, owing to my purism of speech, I could not provide even in the metaphorical sense. So much for the lunch, but the evening dinner has never been to me anything else but the tear-strewn headstone of many hungry hours of hope. It is either a pot-pourri of Parisian phrases, or a still more stand-and-deliver dilemma than the lunch - steak and chips or nothing at all. Indeed I was once so dragooned by steak and chips that I resolved on nothing at all, and in that hour of unfathomable folly repaired to the station hotel hard by. There was an air of 'Sweet Homeland Good-bye' about it, a continual coming and going of travellers, long steaming sighs from the engines, the sudden whistle of departing trains, and then the desolating silences which made of the night a nightmare of suspense. I ordered dinner, and was served with some poor impersonal potatoes that had been boiled and bullied to death hours before, some tired meat that had broken down in the oven, and with them a few very fagged-out vegetables that lay in the death-bed exhaustion of the gravy. And after paying the bill I felt in like case. Really, railway restaurants are a question for the League of Nations.

Is there any escape from the evening steak and chips of the English hotels? This is a perplexity much more to the purpose than the overlaboured problems and the questions over queried of the philosophers. I hope I shall not be accused of self-glorification when I say that on uncounted occasions I have gone with contentment and with some-thing else than steak and chips to bed. The first instance was at Bristol, where I arrived one evening in the last-ditch desperation of either breaking the bank at Brooke Street or of braving a bench all night on the Embankment. What, I asked myself, is the test of a good hotel - and by good I mean where every comfort is to be had, and where you pay the bill dry-eyed. The test in holiday hotels is the state of your boots in the morning, though for the purposes of proof beforehand it is embarrassing to stand at a strange door in order to inspect betimes the boots of those who leave. There are dinner tests, but you have to survive them to know, except when a menu card is displayed at the door. In such an instance you may decide at once, for the measure of any meal is naturally that of its idler items, the first course and the dessert, just as the security of a bank is that of its weakest wall, or the morality of a crowd that of the worst man in it. The first course ought to be an effort, not simply a phrase on the menu, and the dessert should prove the skill of the cook and not the accomplishments of a canner, nor the quality of the confectioner round the corner. In almost every case, however, experience is the price of proof, but at Bristol I proved first, and made a pleasure and not a payment of the experience that followed.

There are few facts in life I remember so well. I had come from the station, and had passed several hotels without so much as a glance, for hotels in Bristol are as common as they are commonplace, and even the finest, which were not frequent, were as featureless as the flow of faces in a London street, and not nearly so homely. In fact I was looking for personality, for, without it, perfection in all else has its price, as such is only a foundling of earth and not a gift of the skies. Character was my quest, and quite by chance I found it. As I was walking along I saw a quiet hotel, and I knew at the first glance that it was the place for me. I stood on the opposite side of the road, naturally not to debate my decision, for that was taken, but just to be certain of the signs, and for an odd minute or two I remained there, as much to indulge my eyes as to alleviate my longings before going in. And the signs? The bedroom curtains, and between, a peep of fresh flowers. Well-kept curtains and fresh-cut flowers! These are the sure indications of a refined hostess and an orderly house. Moreover as I looked across a chambermaid came to the window, and I saw she was not young but old. Old servants and exquisite curtains! My escape from steak and chips and from the drab discomforts of provincial hospitality, from mashed-up meals and high-flyer prices, lay within those walls. She was no common hostess, the hostess of the Grave and Gay as I shall call her, who kept her curtains clean and her servants long. Of course a widower may have old servants, but then the curtains would require others to conceal them. No! there was a hostess there, unique in her kind, and the proof if any were needed lay in the old servant at the window. There must be harmony in a household where women endure each other for years. All women can be angels to men, but the test of a woman is this - is she an angel to women? I do not count it unto her for righteousness if a girl is nice to me. I expect it. But is she nice to other girls? That is the query. So without further demur I strode across the street and in a few seconds I was shaking hands with the sweet-faced hostess of the Grave and Gay. She rang for no maid, but after a word to the boots about my bag she took me up to my room herself. And such a room! Snow white sheets, towels bleached in the sunshine, camphor in the drawers, prim cream curtains, and flowers. And there at long last were all the trifling despairs of a traveller's life, shaving paper, special hook for my strop, waste-paper basket, hangers for my clothes, and a clock if I chose to have one. And what did I like for supper? Yes, Bristol is the queen of the West Country, but there is a queen of Bristol. And she is the hostess of the Grave and Gay.

But that was at Bristol, miles away and years ago, and I am still at Peterborough, which knows of no such amenities, but which is a poor province of the provinces, a parochial spot, with industry enough to make it dreary, inns to make it more so, and with memories which emphasise the mouldiness rather than the eminence of other days. There may be beauties in Peterborough, beauties whose best description is the bliss of them, loveliness that must be lived to be known, but they are all of the Cathedral. There is the fanciful frontage, the

Norman nobility of the nave, the decorated grace of the retro-choir which is a towering triumph of the finer frailties of the human finger and of the enduring delicacy of the eye. They are not beauties however to be borne away. Their majesty is a majesty immured, their charm the charm of a churchyard, where such sedate adornments of nature as the willow, the yew and the cypress show best when affording obscurity. Some pleasing impressions I had, but they were all buried before I left, and if in any spot more profoundly than another in the sanctuary itself. For on either side of the choir, almost hidden away in the heavy shadow of those vaulted aisles, were two graves - graves of perhaps the unhappiest ladies of our written history, Katherine of Aragon and Mary Queen of Scots. Indeed misfortune could have pointed to no apter spot than the sombre aisles of Peterborough Church, nor could have found a more melancholy memento mori than that old solitary austerity of stone. Here was not as at Ely, amid the more stately and sedater tones of art, any of that lyric lightness, any of that vivacity of form and liveliness of line, which, whilst moving the emotions to maturer meditations of life and death, refreshed the fancy, inspired the spirit, and informed the heart with softer thoughts of fate and of futurity, but here all was massive, monastic, mediaeval, where not an arch that bowed over the aisles, not a pier that laboured up into the forbidding dimness of the roof, not a vaulting that weighed down on the walls but did not echo back the unhardened hopes of unhappy hundreds of years, not a stone that did not utter the unuttered tragedy nor speak the unspoken guilt of those two graves, nor mock the glitter of all that regal glory on which they had closed for ever. For here dishonour must await its dimittis in vain.

Held in the dark durance of that old imprisoning pile, graven in the very granite, fettered fast to the unforgetting flags, it endures on with death itself, gathering shame from generation to generation, and touching with the taint of its darkness the sum of all things. Surely it is no effete fancy, no stalemated superstition to wish to lie light and in the open, to be everlastingly leagued with the stones of the field, which have after all a sight of the sun and a measure of immortality. Though deep in the death of other days they are still alive with the movement of the morning, they still feel in the dreariest waste of winter the pulse of the returning spring. The very world is of them and with them, the cycle of the ages is theirs, and even in the exacter science of attraction and emanation they keep their communion with the stars. Perhaps it is the least affliction to be as they when the brief puff is over, and when, free from the fame and from the infamy of our lost lives, we come down to the clods of the valley at last.

CHAPTER FIVE

To Lincoln with pessimist reflections

It is a solace for many of the annoyances of railway travel in England to think of the affliction of those foreigners who, with little of the language and with no inkling of the customs of the country, are left to their first reflections in places to which they never wished to go. Even I have been a prey to such reflections, the nature of which it would be easy to guess and profane to enquire, for I never travel without some mishap or other, and wonder every time how the poor foreigner fares. For there are no state railways in England as in Germany, only a chaos of companies, which are perhaps not so chaotic as they were, but sufficiently so to make a chaos of my calculations. And it is not that I am stupid. Indeed I have always assumed that I am among the most intelligent of men, and certainly should be so if life in general and the railways of England did not prove the reverse. And of this reverse view Peterborough afforded an example.

    I was up betimes to catch the London-York express, for the expresses of England are unique for speed and for punctuality, and he who trusts to a second's grace receives it - with the extra grace of hours waiting for the next. So while paying my bill I reflected that were I relieved of my bag I should not fail to catch the train. Accordingly I said to the proprietor, 'How about my bag?' He looked. 'Ah yes, your bag!' he replied, and called for George. At the very sound a man appeared. He might have grown out of the ground, so silent was his entry, so prompt his response. It was George. Were those my bags? They were. Was I going by the York express? I was. At half past eight? At that very hour. And George shouldered my bag, and went as mysteriously as he had come. I waited for my receipt, and then followed with the added dignity of distance George and the vanished bag. I knew my way to the Station? Of course! Had I not arrived at that station the day before? So I moved off down High Street keeping my eyes open for my bag and for George, but though the High Street was deserted I did not catch a glimpse of him, not even of his shadow. I strained my eyes - to no purpose, I walked more quickly -but in vain. Even from the bridge which looked down on a level stretch of road to the station I saw nothing. Perhaps he went with the bus, I concluded, or by bicycle, or by tram. Who knows the ways of mice and men? No one! and consoled by the ignorance of all, and content with my share of it, I strode on to the station. It was cold, still, deserted. No bag! no George! Oh I shall enquire! and I knocked at the ticket office. 'How about the express to York?' The assistant stared. 'Oh that is at the Great Northern!' 'Great Northern!' I replied, 'but this is the L.N.E.R.' 'Yes, but still the Great Central! The companies are united, but the time-tables are as divided as before.' He advised a taxi. I sprang into one at hand and we were out of the square in a twinkling, up that level road, over the bridge along High Street, round the corner in such a swerve that I almost swallowed my heart, and tore up to the station - in time. The train was steaming in, but glory be! there was the bag, and there was George! And he helped me in.

But what did I give George for his labours? Years ago I used to be over-genial to such men as George, and was very prodigal of my superfluous pence till I was shamed out of extravagance by the great starvation strikes for another half-penny an hour. Since then I have ceased to waste anything on waiters, or on porters, who are in the main little entitled to a gratuity. No one ever goes to the engine-driver with the solace of a sixpence for his very responsible services. No one repairs to the kitchen of a hotel to give what has often been deeply needed and just as deeply deserved, while those to whom we are most indebted, the workers in coal and iron, the labourers on the land, must battle for their bread without our yielding them even so much as the tribute of a sigh. Nowadays I temper my tipping with a little philosophy and the philosophy is this. It is easy to give too much, but it is just as easy to give too little. Moreover in the latter case, if an error has been made, I can give more, but in the former case it is difficult to ask for anything back. My wisdom is therefore to give too little and then to study the countenance of him who serves. I can then proceed to give him not excess but satisfaction. It was so with George. I gave him something, and he took it with such reservation of feeling as showed him to be a personality, and not as most porters, a problem of small change. 'Is your pay included in the hotel bill?' I asked with a little diplomacy. 'Oh no!' he replied. 'Ah, your pardon!' and I gave him something more. He was not effusive. The station did not reverberate with his blessings. But he was satisfied. I knew he was. He waited till the train steamed out and then he bade me a cheery good-bye. And I bade good-bye as well, - to Peterborough, - and to George.

It was just after leaving Peterborough that I was beset by a disturbing thought. I had felt it before, though vaguely, but it now gathered emphasis with the speed of the express, and appeared to grow with the regular and reiterated rhythm of the wheels. I was not on travel, I was in flight. I realised that I had cast my coat among the litter of my illusions in the slums of Ely, and was now pell-mell-ing on to a still more break-neck beyond. Despite my purpose I was seeing nothing, certainly thinking nothing, and to my dismay I found myself just tearing ahead with the sightless stare of the tourist, earmarking names, memories and men, jumbling them together amid many others, and finally putting the flourish of a heartfelt 'for ever' to every good-bye. I had only glimpsed at Ely, I had scamped Peterborough, I was careering on to Lincoln, prepared as I knew for no more than a tripper peep, for an assurance that I had seen it, and for the certainty that I should never by any chance see it again. I know there are many who journey like this, many who allow the tinkling cymbals of their own taste to be lost in the sounding brass of the travelling agencies, who go their way - who see what ought to be seen, who endeavour to know what ought to be known, who come and go, and are satisfied. But I myself had never been hounded on to the highway before. I had always refused to be stampeded to places of tourist interest, to be cat-called into the common chorus, to be jockeyed into a tame indulgence of the general idea. Those who travel in this way must have a hope and a destination, and must be as hardened in the one as they are definite in the other, rigid against any random romance or any poetical caprice of the spirit that might lead them astray. But I am a man without a hope, and in the best and philosophic sense, a man without a destination, one who, in despair of seeing beyond the dead-ends of birth and death, slumbers in a deliberate oblivion of the day after and wakes only with the will to forget his yesterdays.

I must return however to that disturbing thought about which I spoke, and which I have still to explain. It is one of the alleviations of evil to know that it is shared by others and yet there is consolation in being alone in affliction. What is exceptional is accidental and may pass, but where calamities are shared by all no one is so bold as to pray for distinction and hope for special favour. Grief from which no-one is exempt is accepted as a condition of nature, and only ecstasy would aspire to wander beyond the bounds of our being and to walk with God. I had the despair of this reflection after seeing Peterborough and Ely, and when I had contemplated both the mistaken grandeur of what once was and the unmistakable grossness of what is now, and had compared the charge of shame on modernity with the charge of folly on the past, I lost some faith in the elect character of human kind. It was borne upon me that we are the trifles and the toys of the time, and that when the fashion of us is over we are tossed aside. And though I have always room for this misgiving when I come upon some scene of desolation, some old ruin which lies in the solitary wreck of its own forgotten glory, I never had such panic space for doubt as when I saw the great cathedrals which I have just described, and observed the aspiring splendour of lost ages left for ever aspiring and for ever splendid amid the penniless and backstreet unbeauties of to-day. Nor could I deny the thought that some sceptic generation might wonder, when surveying both, which more cumbers the ground.

The disaster of death that attends all endeavour inclines mankind as much to infidelity as to belief. It is natural that the majority in despair of earthly deliverance dispose their thoughts to other and divine interventions, and make a happiness of desponding hopes, and yet there are many who have not the courage to accept the transgressions of the grave. Certainly the dilemma might allow us to believe that the cross we carry is our own credulous good-will to God, and that the crown is a caricature, a pleasantry of the upper powers, or perhaps an uproarious hoax of hell, which when it has tumbled our bones into the mould, draughts us out into the void with the dead dust of our dogmas and with the cobwebs of our conceit, and swirls us along amid the lunary illusions of our race, amid the jesuit caps, the protestant prayers, and the pagan pom-poms, and all the other fleeting ludibria of the limbo. And what is to prove that providence is not gravely pleased to play at pitch and toss with us all, flattering us during our lives into a benevolent view of the universe by favours and by forfeits, and then bundling us off with blanks and oblivion at the close? And who will decide the dilemma between the ugly ease of the present and the laborious loveliness of the past? Are we in our modern ugliness of ease to cry shame on ourselves, or are we at long last beyond the pride and vainglory of those who would spend their lives and ours in tempting the desolations of time? For while the best of us never labour without labouring for the eternities, still even the dreamers will admit that it is a fantastic folly to bake bread for generations yet unborn.

There is naturally one thing which makes fools of us all, and that is time, either from irony by allowing us the pretence of wisdom while we live, or from mercy in revealing our folly only when we have gone. The knowledge of one age is the nodding of the next, the bible of one era is the babble of another, and our grandfathers in the body are our grandchildren in the spirit. In these turmoiling days when belief in everything and belief in anything is a symbol of simplicity, how proud we are to observe that the heresies of yesterday are the commonplaces of to-day, and how tardy to admit that the commonplaces of to-day will be the superstitions of the morrow! Not one truth, not one ideal, not one God we have but has feet of clay. Their golden heads must at some time go toppling in the dust. And that is the whole of our human story - the open hand to us when we come, and fingers to the nose when we go. We may march to the horizon as we will, the horizon is always a march beyond, and though we go from strength to strength we are never stronger; though we go from wisdom to wisdom we are never wise. Every day is as long as the one before it, every year is as long as the last. And so we tramp through the round of them all, toiling on and toiling eternally on the never-ending treadmill of time. But I think this is pessimism!

CHAPTER SIX

Something of Lincoln

If these were my thoughts on leaving Peterborough they were my obsessions in Lincoln round which I was wandering some hours later. I suppose there are few towns in England more ancient than Lincoln, few where one perceives in brief such a large perspective of our history. It claims the most early associations, Celtic, Latin, and Anglo-Saxon, and was the seat of a Roman Colony, a plundered prize of the Danes, a favoured stronghold of William the Conqueror. And history has not been silent since. But it is all a manuscript magnificence, a guidebook glory which points a moral but does not adorn the town. For at Lincoln the contrasts are crasser than at Ely, and the ill-assortment of the centuries serves to portray the pranks of providence in an even greater degree than the progress of mankind.

Such was my view after I had climbed the lofty steep on which the old castle stands, and had looked out on to the modern mediocrity of the town below. It was a fresh and blowy day, enlivened by sudden sweeps of sunshine, drifting cloud shadows, and short gusts of occasional rain. There was not a breath of mist and I could see beyond the town the long pastoral stretches of the Lincolnshire low-lands which lay under a wide amplitude of sky clear and green to the horizon. Down to my left was the Cathedral, standing gravely erect and proudly perpendicular against the tumbled riot of cloud behind, in appearance very mediaeval and very monumental, and, in contrast with the landscape, as mute and as unmoved as the dead who lay buried in the close. The eye could not fail to wander back to it as it stood there so storied over with the stately and sequestered dignity of other days, so rich in the numerical grace of its insetted front, in its decorated detail, in its unique and elegant length of line. The impression was of something supremely separate, something superbly apart both from the bluster of the wind above and from the rabble of the rakish roofs below, something aloofly patrician and still as of one who is musing with his memories alone. But far away to my right was life, a vigorous flood of it. For there was the racecourse, thronged and throbbing with the press of humanity, ringing with the roar of it, alive with ramping horses, jubilant jockeys, and pavilions brightly ablaze with pennants and flags. There was Lincoln, the Lincoln of to-day, the loud and living Lincoln. It was there that present blood was pulsing, that fellow hearts were beating, and that modern minds were stirred, but stirred with never a thought for the forgotten fury that once raged round that ancient castle wall, nor for the fast-dying drama that is still re-echoed in the old cathedral choir.

Yes, Lincoln is a place of contrasts, and the contrast so evident in the people themselves was reflected in the town. Right up to the racecourse and beyond it were long lines of meagre modern houses, tiny dots of red and white standing out amid the greenery like the dabs on a painter's palette, architectural mushrooms Uttered in the shadow of the long-standing oaks of the middle-age, the merest butterfly buildings flitting round the mountainous mammoths of the past. There everything was cheap and easy, and everything where I stood permanent and impossible. I was hovering there on that lofty castle wall between the littleness of life and the grandeur of death, between living days and buried years, and as I looked on these tiny items of time daisied amid the outstanding tracts of eternity I was oppressed by a prejudice against my own age. At least I thought so, but any doubts I may have had were resolved in a chat with a friend. He lives in such a house as I saw, a small and modern one, unclassical and cheap. His answer to a casual criticism of mine was decisive. 'Were I Tutankhamen, with thoughts of eternal tombs and of repose till the resurrection, I might agree, but my purpose in life is not the pyramids of Egypt.' He had a choice between a big house with imprisonment in it, or a small house and a car, and his choice was not delayed. Imprisonment, however splendid, made no appeal beside humility and the open air. So every week-end he is over the hills and far away, and never is he seen again till he returns on Monday morning.

Perhaps there is something of relativity in this, some feeling that there is no fixed standard after all, that there is nothing permanent on earth, and that if love and labour are to be lost they are better lost on ourselves. In the rough and tumble of these times we have learned to gather the rosebuds while we may, and we no longer let them bloom in posthumous days to gild the glamour of other people's hours. Naked we come and naked we go, and we are at last alive to the vanity of our own undress while making swaddling clothes for the unborn and shrouds ad lib for the dead. Houses shrink in size, motors multiply, and realising that we must be as fleet as time itself to catch its joys, we break with the old static truths and pass on into moving modernity. Indeed to those who have felt the more newly revealed facts that the hills are afloat, that the earth is in a flux, and that the world itself is a wanderer, there is no folly like to that which would build a pyramid on final foundations, or would erect a Babel to touch the stars. For this is the folly of 'Thus far and no further' in life, the folly that would moor in the open main, or that would hitch one's bark to the howl of the wind.

    Yet the bogey of the big building, the monstrous mumbo-jumbo of the past, the ponderous spirit of the Pyramids of Egypt still lie like press-yard stones on the breast of the present day. I was repelled by this superstition some years ago in the Brera Gallery of Milan. Now, going through a gallery is like going down a hill, you gather motion as you go. You survey the first room with deep devotion, and the second also you inspect with devotion. Of hardly more than ordinary depth, the third evokes nothing but interest, you lounge through the fourth, you stride through the fifth, slip the sixth, and then, bundling all pretence to the winds, regardless of masterpieces, reckless of names which inspired heartbeats and bated your breath when you read of them in books, you career on, ignoring guides and missing rooms, and speed up, with tired eyes and a cricked neck, into a Nurmi-like velocity at the door. Now this was my experience at the Brera which I entered with thoughts of art and left with demonstrations of speed. The first room was full of Madonnas, and to my dismay the second room was also full - of Madonnas, and the third room had more Madonnas than the second, and the fourth room had more Madonnas than the third. And there were twenty-eight rooms. I have never gazed into a girl's eyes since. I never see a woman with a child without turning away with such a twinge in my neck and such a weariness in my eyes as perhaps bespeaks my overwrought nerves. The very memory is a solace for celibacy, a spur to those austerities of life which empty the land and make highways of the wilderness.

No, the Brera, like every gallery of art, is a majestic and monumental mistake, a big something which serves more to flatter the pride of the city than to inform the spirit of the world. They not only fail of their purpose; they defeat it, and their aim will never be attained because pictures have become idols of adoration and not instruments of culture as they should be. Thus galleries have become temples and not workshops, shrines and not schools of art. They are closed in the evening when men have time, and are remote from such as would enjoy them, while those who have the wealth to journey there and enter have not the wisdom to be wiser when they leave. But if art really lies in concealing art then I shall confess to a calumny.

If mankind is to be served then the galleries must be levered from their foundations and the pictures must be put on wheels. Here is a solution which would eliminate the museums one rarely sees, and would recompense painters who are in want of sales. Societies, and there are records of such, might be formed, and instead of a gallery of pictures the members would have a lending library of art. No paintings would be sold, they would be loaned. They would be brought and hung up in the members' homes, where they could see them, study them, enjoy them, use them. And when they visited their friends they would be faced not by trash from which they would turn away, but by pictures, masterpieces, works of art. And every month they would have a new one, to refresh their fancy, to temper their taste, to retune the tones of their thought. 'But' cries the static mind, 'the masterpieces would be ruined by use, they would become old, broken, and our joy in them would be over!' Naturally! And when they are old, when they are broken, when we no longer have any joy in them, what then? Well? Well then to the flames with them! For we shall never be the heirs of the world till the old lords are dead.

That man is the first interest of man, and not the work of his hands, and that the present has precedence over the future and over the past are the most subversive of all subversive ideas. It is certain that they brought Christ himself to the grave, for it was not his disparagement of the Pharisees but his disrespect of the Temple that occasioned the charge and confirmed the judgment. No wonder when he told the high priests that their synagogues, their sacrifices, their prayings, their washings, their elaborate ritual and complicated cult were not to the purpose, that Jerusalem itself was a trumpery of tradition, and that where two or three were gathered together there was a church, no wonder when he said these things that they hurried him to the gallows. I do not doubt that those who worship him to-day, would, were they to know the drift of his idea, hurry him to the gallows once more.

But this word of the gallows brings me back to Lincoln, back to the old castle walls, which have themselves a gallows and a glut of graves. From the observatory tower I could see the sites of both. To the north-east was that of the gallows, a heavy Edwardian stronghold that rose in all its rank and rakehell irony in full flaunting view of the Cathedral front and of the eastern sky, and to the southwest was that of the graves which lay, by an irony no less rank and rakehell, in the Keep. For there is no secretive shame in either, thrust as they are on to the topmost pinnacles of the castle, and yet within easy compass of the cloister and the vibration of the bells. It would seem therefore no anomaly in Christian ethics to return men to God flat to His face, to reject them in the very blast of His breath as fitter for His company than for ours, to answer their shrieks by canticles of goodwill, and to subdue our re-echoing conscience by the deep and many-chorded harmonies of Jesu Lover of my Soul, and, by God's condescending grace - Lover of the souls of those we have downed. Let us be devout in the shadow of the groves, and in the overarching greenery of the green trees, but let our altars and our offerings be in the high places where we may show our mercy to man and our gratitude to God by giving back the souls He gave. And who are our victims to complain? By prayers they are sped, with a sprinkle they have sanctity, with a little soil - a viaticum, and in the headstone is a valediction to their deed and to ours. Some water, and what hands more clean? some time and what memories more calm? a hymn or two, what hearts more uplifted? a sign of the cross, and our souls are as safe as a body under the sod. For in the nod of the Lord's anointed, and in the sanction of the surplice is our dispensation, and given these, we may - when in livery - despoil millions of their days, and yet hope for the more abundance, both to them and to ourselves in eternity.

I came down from the observatory tower, crossed the courtyard, and went up a stone causeway to the Norman Bastion high on the mound. There was a narrow entrance but no view either back into the castle or forward into the country beyond. It was just a gloomy compound, girt in by embattled walls, and, save for the dank shadow of some straggling trees, open to the sky. There before me were low headstones, and therein unkempt and unconsecrated neglect were the graves. Two or three ragged rows, mossed and moulded over, a driven litter of rotting leaves, a smother of dishevelled ivy and that was all. And so I came away.

Macaulay in his History of England has a passage touching the burial of the Duke of Monmouth, who lies in the chapel of St. Peter in the Tower. 'Indeed, says Macaulay, 'there is no sadder spot than that little cemetery,' and then takes note of the many eminent men who met their death on the scaffold, and who were buried in that tragic vault. Notable names they are, of historical interest and of illustrious association, names whose soaring ascendancy is in calamitous contrast with their fall. But humility has its tragedies no less deep, and this burial spot of those who went down with dirty hands and in darkness to their graves has a sadness beyond that of the Tower. For there is no aristocracy in grief, no privilege of purple in the aches of the heart, and though certain blood may plume itself on its blueness, common salt is the scalding quality of all tears. The characters of Macaulay's rhetorical parade had drunk of sweeter cups in life. Their lips touched bitterness only in their last hours. But in Lincoln lie those to whom the cup of bitterness was a daily portion and a birthright, who perhaps had known no other pleasure but freedom from pain, and who never even lived in the twilight of hope before entering the ignoble night of despair. Theirs was the mere shaking of the olive tree of life, the niggard gleaning of the grapes when the full-blooded vintage was over, and their passage in death was from ashes to sackcloth and ashes, and from dust to dishonoured dust and the dirt.

I have more notes which I wrote of Lincoln, but which, touching only myself and my own aimless wanderings, might have been written elsewhere. The Castle, the Cathedral, the antiquities, and the racecourse, these were my public pensum, systematically seen and rigorously recorded, and, though I say it, forgotten when finished. This performed, I lapsed into a more leisurable style, knowing nothing of history, science, and art in my strolls, neither consulting Baedeker nor rummaging my memory, but vacantly seeing what I saw and innocently hearing what I heard, and entrusting the intimacies to my notes. I had a letter of introduction to a person of some standing in the town, but I burned it, flicking the ashes up the chimney with an alleviation of heart, such as only they can know who talk rather to men than to the education of them. For after long acquaintance with the so-called cultured, I have concluded that the proper place for most of those who are lettered is on a hayrick, or pitchforking in the compost as symbolic of themselves and of their studies, or - perhaps as still more symbolic - hobnailing it along the highway. Alone in such a station is the farmyard finesse of their philosophy, and - what is worse in my eyes - the corduroy elegance of its expression, in good bucolic keeping with everything else. As it is, the apex of our academic pyramid is not he who is endowed with the things of the spirit, who has something to give, something beyond the banal portion of the press of men, but he who has the biggest pen, the most paper, and an unbridled passion for print, one whose sole desire is to be seen on the shelf, and whose destiny is to be left there. And above my prejudice against those educated is a prejudice, as precipitate as that of St. Paul, against education itself. It might have its uses, its abuses are known to us all. With it stupidity is easily defended, collapses from grace cushioned up, and pretence to divine favour plausibly proved. And where all have learned the lesson by rote who is to know the magpie from the master? who is to see in the largesse of language the dearth of idea? in the fulness of knowledge the want of wisdom? in the ripple of dress the dummy beneath? The schools may have given us mental battledores by the million, but there is one standardised shuttlecock for them all.

I remember taking my way amid the litter of the wharf to the canal bank, to the further and less frequented side, and talking to the bargees who literally lived in the moorings. There was one who had made his skiff into a floating home, and who never stepped ashore save to buy in food, and to contract with those whose barges he steered. And every week-end when work was over, or on the odd days when trade was still, he was always to be found at Lincoln stowed away in his tiny cask of a cabin, having no company but that of his pipe and no occupation but that of his own toy thoughts. He had lived in a house once with his wife and child, but it was like the wide house of the Proverbs, and moreover, used as he was to his little hutch aboard, it was so windy that the open prairie could not have been less cheerful. A few weeks in this wild wilderness of a home and then - he had returned to his nutshell moorings in Lincoln, to his tiny tea-cup cabin, where the fire was within a span of his knees, and where he had but to stretch his arm and everything from the roof to the floor was at his hand. His very seat was both the lid of a chest and a bed-board, every panel in the walls was a locker, every plank in the floor a door to deeper things. He explained each in turn, and then passing all in review in one rapt and revolving glance, he addressed himself to the fire, and proved his skill as cook and his heart as a host by making a massive meal of meat and potatoes without leaving the spot on which he sat. This he accomplished all by himself, and afterwards from the one plate and with a spoon apiece we set to, I in gratitude to him and he in goodwill to me and the world.

Yet for all his open and simple innocence I felt there was a sadness in his life, the sadness of one astray in the solitudes of his own soul. He was lonely, and of that loneliness which comes of inner darkness, for owing to heavy misfortune he had long since shut the door on himself and on the light of his days. Perhaps he felt at home within, but the casement was closed, the blind was drawn, and the lamp had not been kindled. Indeed he had so hugged his narrow hearth that he had never known the wider home of the world, but tarried on in the twilight of untravelled thoughts, and in the dusk of his dwindling ideas, meeting in men only strange men, seeing only unfamiliar faces, and hearing in voices none that re-echoed his own. He might in the heavily halting hours of the evening take a peep from his cabin top, press his face against the little poop window, and peer out into the darkness, but all that he saw was a waste beyond, mysteries of movement, a dark argosy of life as it were drifting swiftly past the shallows of his little care-free anchorage, and leaving him alone with the unceasing sound of the surge and with the cry of the gulls. He knew that life was passing, that the hand of Heaven had never been open though often raised against him, that he had neither name nor genealogy in the universe, that he was an unnoted one in the unnumbered many, but nevertheless with a half-pagan, half-believing piety owed the humility of thanks even in being as the dust. Many in his case would have charged God or challenged humanity, but he was resigned, and with the unworded wisdom of the sucklings rejoiced in what pleasures he had and left his sufferings to time. In this he was certainly my master, for it is the first and last earnest of all happiness to have in the fulness of humiliation the understanding of thanks, to be loyal to one's lot, and despite titles, rank, possessions, and power, to feel oneself, in the simple lineage of grief and gladness, a king. Naturally there are men, and of such I do not doubt he was one, who in all heroism are bowed for the burden, who trudging under the drudgery of long-dragging days have no other word but that of agreement with God, and who in the peace of pain, in the privileged peace of bitterness bitterly borne, are happy even to endure. And if ever our hearts are light it is because our shoes are heavy with the dust of them.

Next day I was bidding good-bye to Lincoln, and taking a distant look at the commanding Cathedral and at the Castle crowned by the gallows and the graves, but I caught no glimpse of the skiff which in the early morning had gone from the canal. Somehow I went there again, wedged my way over the wharf, and then wandered along the brambled path to the canal bank. The moorings, however, were deserted, the capstans were clear, and I turned away back by the towing path to the town. I was not disappointed for I had scarce expected to see my companion of the day before, or to board the skiff which was well away by now over the far flats of the Lincolnshire Plain. I thought of going up to the Castle wall once more, and sighting the sail, for the sky was blue and the sun was shining clearly, but I shuddered when I remembered the unshakable shadows on the hill. I had no longer eye nor heart for the stagnant darkness of death, but in very contrast was eager for a glimpse of a far-off and frail sail afloat in the wind, for a living glint of white straining bravely forward like the swaying widespread wings of a gull stemmed against the storm. For with it, in my companion, was an exalted symbol, a portrait, though only in its plainer features, of myself. Perhaps I have roamed too long with the wild asses of the philosophic wilderness, have grazed too indiscreetly on the gorse and couch grass of academics to find a delight in the green pastures and still waters which are in the common gift of nature. Indeed I fear I shall never attain those truths which are truisms to simpler souls. There are many who lose and find again, but I am one who, after many days of darkness and years of seeming exile, have lost the pearl and found only the price.

CHAPTER SEVEN

Something of sarcasm (Sheffield and Liverpool)

It was on leaving Lincoln that I began to have some ado with my diary. The first few pages had been very precise, and as to inner feelings so exact and so exacting a confessional, that I was open to embarrassments, if not to blushes, whenever rny book chanced to be mislaid. In fact I scarce dared to glance at them myself, and every time I made a note I would skip the pages over like the leaves of a ledger with blank unconcern, and with the pretence that all was as it should be. Later on however my notes were such that my embarrassments began to be bearable, and my blushes were reserved rather for the emptinesses than for the entries which, as they lacked the impulsive blood of the confessional grape, might have been proclaimed from the steeples without the raising of an eyebrow. It was as though after one crowded market-day of the emotions, my stocks of intimacy had run low, and an enduring exhibition, a long-drawn-out Leipzig Fair of the feelings was not to be thought of. I was distressed at this inner dearth, for confession is the touchstone of all thought. Indeed science is nothing but the full avowal of ourselves one to another, the united total of widespread experience personally expressed and universally noted, and valid only when truly declared. And they are wisest who, as heirs of the lives of others, honestly disclose their own.

I might have spared my repinings had my journal been full of what I had seen and heard, or had I conveyed even some of the interest of travel into what I wrote. But when I arrived in Sheffield my pen was a burden, and, what is more, a burden of such banalities as I happened to blob on the page, and as bespoke neither what was done without, nor felt within. There are times as Johnson says when the hand is out, but the glut of commonplace which I crowded into my pages, the derelict dottings of half-attempted thoughts that alternated with niggard notes on the turmoil of the streets and on public bustle, had perhaps another reason. Looking at my diary I saw that I might enlarge with ease on the littleness of Ely, that I might be prodigal of paper, if not of philosophy, on the poverty patch of Peterborough, and even elaborate Lincoln into a lengthened legend of my own life and still have length and legend to spare, but with my first step into Sheffield, and with every succeeding step to Manchester and Liverpool, I was in bonds, in the fetter of that ac velut in somnis feeling so well described by Virgil, when our leaping limbs languish away beneath us, when our voice falters in our failing breath, when we wish to scream and are silent, when we would struggle, though thought, speech and spirit are still. I was on the cross of 'I must and I cannot': and whatsoever reflections, feelings, and impressions I entertained, irrespective of how they were occasioned and of how often they were recalled, all were jumbled into the like jingleese, the reflections for lack of a matter worth remembering, the feelings for want of a depth to indulge them, the impressions for the absence of that personal appeal which is at once their preservation and preserve. And I had only to take a note of them to realise that I was not noting them at all.

Now one view, my first and, as it happened, my last of Sheffield, involves everyone. It was from Victoria Station and as I looked through the smother of the smoke, through the driving dust and floating petrol-fumes into the obscurity of the city beyond, as I saw the dingily stacked-up streets stretching into the blur of the background, the waste of warehouses, the grimy rout of roofs, chimneys, factories, posts, and placards I wondered if I could have any other thoughts than one. The more I saw, whether of the city itself or of the steel mills and blast-furnaces outside, the more my wonder grew. For I knew that I was less among men than among the work of their hands, less among my fellows than in a flush of faces where each was lost as a shadow in the general darkness, that I was listening less to familiar voices than to the unfamiliar volume of them, to the repetitive roar of the kettle-drumming treadle of industry, to the common echo of the grand auctioneering hammer of capitalism on the skulls of my kind. Here time, which is the very sanction of ourselves, and the ulterior sanctity of all our hopes and despairs, was ticked off on clocks and docketed as turnover in the tills. Here was humanity, men, women, and children, whom philosophy and faith have elevated to the first and favourite place under the skies, harnessed beneath the hard iron of an unyielding yoke, their expectations heaped under the hotch-potch of profits, their disappointments dumped a-mid the unprofitable dross of debts. Here, and more so in the clanging steel mills than elsewhere, were eyes as blank as the uncurtained panes of workhouse glass, here were faces as featureless as the regimented bricks in the factorywall, ears that heard a dithyramb in the dinnerhorn, tongues that touched their highest delight in the dinner-hour. And yet here were men, drudges of destitution and of dirt, with their unflinching shoulders to the wheel of the world, women with the air of the wastrel worst about them but honourable still, children with the pap of Babylon in their bones but with growing hearts and hands to help us all. It is a desolating thought for those of us who have a privileged and more pleasured portion in life, that - to use the words of Isaiah - the faces are ground and the flesh is flayed of others to pay the price.

It is however both a query and a criticism, which one cannot forbear after slumming it through the shabbiness of Sheffield, why Britain should spend her beauty abroad. Why does she export her best and keep the worst to mend? make parlours for other people, backyards for herself?' The thought first occurred to me some years ago in Gothen burg, which is a busy port, and yet one, without a paradox, of patrician splendours, with boulevards, gardens and avenues, but above all glorying in many graces which are the gift of Englishmen. It was perhaps to be expected of the English colony there, for an Englishman has a pride in his home, and moreover is wanting neither in public spirit nor in the wherewithal to express it. Indeed it would be difficult to find in England itself any public park of note, any higher seat of learning, any library, any place of worship, any asylum either for the sick or the insane which is not in a measure endowed, and which does not bear witness to someone's success as a merchant and to his sacrifices as a citizen. To a degree unequalled anywhere else the private name is written large on public works and not a year passes without some anonymous instance where the conscience of all is saved from shame by the gift of one. With such a spirit, and rejoicing as we do in the resources to sustain it, why are even our choicest cities like slum suburbs of New York, where the dirtiest chimney sets the tone, and where destitution of taste contends with decay of trade to placard our poverty of both to the world? Need industry dictate us to the dustbin? Must business privately pocket the profits and publicly tip the refuse? And should finance whilst lavishing investments in the boulevarded beauty and tourist attractiveness of the Southern Hemisphere, make us a nodding of the head and a holding of the nose to all the nations? And ought those whose labour keeps them in the town, and whose pleasure is what they chance upon in it, to be content as in Sheffield with the minor amenities of Weston and Kenwood Park, with factory-polluted peeps of the pleasant uplands beyond, and with the poor and pent-up hopes of a more spacious scene free to the foot and open to the eye, when the 'ifs' have ceased from troubling, and the 'buts' are finally at rest?

I do not know which is the less agreeable, to receive such impressions as a traveller or to recall them as a diarist. The former displeasure is the greater, but the latter endures, and so in this dilemma of discontents I forgot my thoughts of Manchester, and my thoughts of Liverpool I borrowed from abroad. Not that foreign thoughts are fairer, more exactly conceived or better expressed, but Liverpool was for long years my home, and in quoting a stranger I may lay claim to that gift of the Gods, which was the prayerful petition of Robert Burns, of seeing ourselves as others see us. It was in a book of English scenes, and they were some three hundred in number, taken (as was emphasised in the foreword) less with a view to art than to fact, and published not as studio performances but as truthful impressions, as something typical of England and of its people. Such a reservation might be intended, I admit, either to confirm the deformity of England or to excuse the blunders of the photographer, and one might with reason believe that the author, having failed in his task, has sought by a paraded love of truth to cover his patent lack of taste. But I have reasons for thinking him honest.

Now among these views was one of Liverpool, not a view of the Landing Stage which to the Mersey people is an unnumbered wonder simply because prior to the first, nor indeed St. George's Hall which, in the same conceit, is a welter of all wonders, and which, being perhaps the corner-stone that the builders rejected, was thus omitted from the original list, nor finally of the Delphi Hotel which out wonders wonder itself in being thought to be a wonder at all. It was a view of none of these, but of something we all see and never notice. It was a cross view from the library steps. To the right was the pretentiously pillared portico of the Museum with its tiers of terraced steps to the street below, and beyond, in guttersnipe contrast with all this bigwig banality, was the centre, soul, and cynosure of the whole scene, the unlovely latrines and dubious junk of the Old Haymaker, all wallowing against a setting of ramshackle roofs, shabby shops, and toss-pot pubs, and all looking both in fact and in spirit like bedraggled driftwood awash against the pier. Naturally there was not a glimpse of the sky, but only a swathe of smoke where the sky might have been, an overhanging cast of grime and of greyness, which, clouding out every contrast of colour, might serve to make work a weariness, time a tribulation, and life an elegy to all condemned beneath it. Such was the picture in this book of views, the impression of one who, without bias, embitterment, or preconception, saw Liverpool as a passer-by. He was not a stone's throw from St. George's Hall: he must have seen it both outside and in; and yet he must have reflected that St. George's Hall was a building and not a city, an item singular in itself but not typical of the town, a sort of prize horse eternally trotted out for show while the stable door is being discreetly locked on the pack of staggered nags inside. And he must have reflected moreover that there is something else in the mountain than the peak, and that though the summit is the most visible it is the least in bulk and the last in importance of the mountain's magnificence. So he mingled his admirations, diluted his enthusiasms with the allaying Thames of truth, and proved that the quality of the Mersey was not strained by disclosing some of the dirt that was in it.

And yet he might have refined on refinement. He might have riddled his ironies by giving St. George's Hall as it is, and then without contrast or combination have left it to the unjaundiced judgment of those to whom greatness is better as a characteristic of idea than of size. As with men so with buildings. We judge them both not by their girth but by their character, a thing which to the unimpassioned observer is as difficult to mistake as it is to acquire. For whilst a fool is pleased to expose his nature, a wise man is content to express it, disclosing depths rather than displaying surfaces, and seeking more to make an example of his conduct than an exhibition of himself. And this thought, so true of man, is true of all his works, tritely true of St. George's Hall which is just a show of stone, not a revelation of reflective art, and which, being nothing but a big imposition, is in style simply colossal, in inspiration as blank as a barndoor, and in utility about as useful when there is nothing in the barn. There are indeed buildings such as our own grand and stately St. Paul's where we have but to look around to see not merely the monument but the personality of him who made it, buildings which, having been for long, long years the unspoiled beauty-pieces of indulged and indulgent genius, reveal in the featureless flat of the flattest stone the living face of the artist, in the abstract of his art the earnest of his humanity. Even in the silence of the aisles we hear a fellow footfall, a familiar voice which calls us from our rank-and-file reflections to pace for a while with priority of step and precedence of spirit those walks of the soul which arc so many silent strides ahead of our own. From the highways and the byways of our plebeian selves we are brought in, the wedding garment is ours for the taking, we are plied with the wine of the word, we are favoured with the venison of the spirit, our tongues are loosed, our faces uplifted, our hearts enlarged, and the host himself, a very king, a God that was given, casts his crown and puts his freely beggared hand into ours. For are we not partners of his privilege, guests of his inner communion, sharers of himself from the first fruits of youth to the viaticum of age, and is not the first of hosts he who stops not at the open hand but opens his heart also? But there are those who hire servants to receive us, who have borrowed much of the bounty that awaits our coming, and bought the rest, who have haggled with the harpists to play for the hour and not for the evening, and who to save the cellar turn out the lights at twelve. The failings are not of their own flock, the wine is not of the tillage of their own hands, and above all the whipped-up talk, stilted laughter, and music to order, comes the grating from the kitchen as the cook opens the cans. Finally when the condensed milk of their kindness has been spent, and the last guest has been unctuously valedicted into the outer darkness that is denser than when he came, they gladly glimpse into the accounts, and who will question the joy of the lord that they are still intact? Who will care? And what digestion is turned on knowing that the ewe lamb was pilfered seeing there was good cheer when it was devoured? This is a parable of hosts and it is a parable of artists, a parable of the host and artist of St. George's Hall who was more ambitious of giving of his most than of his best. Indeed just as those talk much who have little to say, so he piled on what it was not in his own power to give. He had bricks - to build a pyramid, mortar - to submerge himself and all his men, wood - to stock a forest. Plans - in plenty on tick from the past, and personality? Oh that was lent by the lookers-on. Of course there is a distinction hairbreadth to some unsubtle souls, between architecture on the one hand and accumulation on the other, just as there is a distinction equally subtle and hairbreadth between a tailor and a clothier, between portrait painting and limewashing walls, between a first-class surgery and a knacker's yard. It may be a platitude, but one does not become classical by lionising in the lumber of Greece and Rome, nor greater as an architect by exhausting the quarries, nor an exemplar of art by baggage-muling the beauties of it. If a simple tree, lovely in the early grace of its greenery, could be cursed for cumbering the ground, is it unkind to hope for no better fate for something which has known neither the grace nor the green of natural nobility, for a building big and banal as a schoolboy's ambition, for an ungainly copybook anticlimax of misapplied time, labour and stone? There are artists as Carlyle says who ought to be carrying a hod, but were they obliged to shoulder the hods they have compelled others to carry, justice would be better served.

But perhaps I am uncivil, perhaps profane, in following the example of the architect himself and casting stones and dust on to the common pile. I say profane, for if a churchyard is proof of a church surely the monumental God's acre of St. John's Gardens is argument of a temple, as in fact the form of the Hall might suggest and the reverence for it confirm. It is certainly kept in such well-curtained seclusion that cynics who are ignorant of the city and of its inner sanctities have asserted that no one knows what to do with the Hall, save when the organ is played, men are hanged, and prizes given to children from the schools. And they assert further that the unbreathed air of some eleusynian something in and around it, the barred and bolted privacy and police-constabled aloofness are simply nothing else but the smug and sabbath isolation of a greengrocer's parlour to serve as an envy to enemies and as a proof of 'going one better' to friends. But this cynicism I no longer share, not since I paced the local valhalla at the back, or St. John's Gardens as it is called, and paid my troubled tribute of a slump of sighs to each of the statues in turn. Indeed no one who has ever communed in this internment camp of the one-time eminent, this open-air Chamber of Honours which is opened in the mornings that recollections might be renewed and closed at night lest they should be lost, can fail to praise the City Fathers, who, having given a cemetery for mortal remains, give a civic churchyard for the immortal masquerade to boot. How happy the citizens of Liverpool must be who have a church as the refuge of their bodies after death, and St. George's Hall as a refuge of their reputations after it! And how much happier must they be than the unfortunates of other towns, who in every street and in every open space are faced by statues more tear-provoking than the departure of them they attempt to portray. For there are many among us, and St. John's Gardens is testimony of it, who smother the remembrance of those they are at pains to bury, and who, moreover, having ensured the best epitaph of their own memories by writing one on their friends, erect a rock of offence for all future judgment to fall over. But from this peril the citizens of Liverpool, by their unique idea of a concentration camp for the unbreathing bronze, have been happily preserved.

But, after all, things of taste are the toys of time, and when their tyranny is over they are tossed aside like the wild flowers of Maying days. There is some sadness in the thought, as bearing on the brevity of our lives, but also some joy, for here is the assurance that enormities are not eternities and that their portion as well as ours is the dust. Years ago it was the unspoken superstition of the people of Liverpool that when the grand resurrection trump sounded, its last awakening echoes would be heard in the porticoed privacy of St. George's Hall. But that was years ago. And now there is a new superstition, whispered first as a hope and proclaimed afterwards as a promise, that the final resounding rounds of the great reveille would be relayed to the new Cathedral. For this is a building 'for all time', even for times which have tired of it, even for the never-never ages when Macaulay's New Zealander, multiplied into American tripper millions, sits amid the crumbling walls or strays among the tumbled stones as in the waste of his own whys and wonders, or lingers at the alpha and omega slab as at some neglected and long-forgotten grave. Out of the destitution of these times, when daily bread is a prayer and a problem of untold thousands, when children are cheaper than the stuff to clothe them, and when pence is the reply to an appeal for pounds, a challenge to the everlasting hills has gone forth, a flourish in the face of futurity. With the frail sponge of an all-absorbing faith we shall mop up the tide in the affairs of men, with the apple of our eyes we shall wink back ciphered centuries to the stars. Having emptied God out of our hearts we shall house Him on the hill-top, where haply posterity may see Him, and where in the ecstasy of our example He may be immured with all the amenities for evermore. And what better pastime for the First of Fathers than to ponder over the perplexities of ecclesiastical ethics, to peruse the Memorial Book to His forty thousand sons who fell and felled others in His name, or to hide His forehead and His eyes in the tattered flags which are hung up as symbols of the bloody shreds in which we are pleased to rend our kind? And what better consolation for the helpless Almighty, when meditating these massacre memorials in honour of the Prince of Peace, to know that, while forgiveness and forgetfulness are preached, forget`fulness at least is practised? Perhaps however after being breezed about in the spacious emptiness of that vast and vaulted vanity of dumb stone, He may sigh to lay His head somewhere in the slums outside, somewhere in the sprawling squalors of the smoke-benighted city, which, it seems, are all that ever endure in the shadow of the church. But this He will abandon to the pretenders to possess it, resign it as a joy to the bats and to the screech-owls of ecclesiastical darkness, to the crows to live there, to the satyrs to dance there, and doubtless in the words of the prophet her days shall not be prolonged.

Still there are many gusts of heterodoxy coursing through the church, and much dust of dogma and many cobwebs of the credo are being draughted out through the great porch door. A spirit of the early catholicity is alive, a broader and more embracing outlook as of the Middle-Age, ultra-montane in the figurative sense of spanning the barrier of unbelief, and assuming all, whether communicants of the Church or not, to be of the fold. I entered the Lady Chapel one afternoon just as the last notes of the organ were vibrating down the nave. The bishop spoke but not of religion. His address was on art which he held to be a handmaid of the faith. There was no scriptural text, nor indeed any references to the Testaments, save in those choice associations of speech which come of long biblical study. He quoted from Tennyson and from Wordsworth, and with the thought that every serious artist is in a measure a Christian Father, appealed to the humanity and not just to the Anglican cast of his hearers. It was an address such as all might have heard, attractive to a secular, refreshing to a religious mind, as removed from the mud-flats of sermonising as it was clear from the thickets of controversy and recrimination, an address which made one conscious of the agreements and dead to the differences among us, and which without drumming of texts offered the influence of the scriptures and their devotional tone. Though an outsider I felt myself no stranger in the congregation, and experienced also a further fellowship in the thought that the voices of our own poets might with little incongruity be added to the graver accents of the prophets of Judaea. Not that I would depreciate the Testaments. Indeed it is sad that the bible with its enduring dignity of diction and with its untouchable chastity of thought should have fallen so low among us, but what other fate was to be expected after the gridiron exegesis of the ecclesiastics and the blind bandying of passages by the drum-head evangelists of later days? Science after all must be served, the last issues of criticism accepted and confessed, the fact faced, as it finally must be, that God has never never lapsed from that superb austerity of silence which He still preserves. When we ourselves boast of buttonholing the Almighty, how may we close the door on the ragamuffin revelations of the spiritualists of to-day? And why should it be bathos and blasphemy to believe that God, after the unspoken seclusion of brain-cracking billions of years, has finally let the cosmic cat out of the bag in Mr Dennis Bradley's back parlour, or broken the age-long barrier of the skies to tell Mr Blatchford about pains in his back?

It seems ungracious to leave Liverpool without speaking of the river, which is the first impression and most lasting recollection of all who visit the town. It seems equally ungracious to neglect the parks and gardens, which in expanse if not in prettiness are without comparison in the provinces. And perhaps a third ungrace might be added in my silence on the great and current schemes of the city engineer, which, had they been early, might have spared Liverpool all her present grossness and certainly much of her future expense. But I am afraid lest I should mingle the impressions of boyhood with later thoughts, and should recall a Liverpool that enlarged most on itself and least on its loveliness, and that, spreading on all sides like the smoke from its chimneys, gauged its greatness by the height of the stacks and its prosperity by how much they belched forth. There has been an entrance of the humanities since then, for as I observed in my diary the younger worker is no longer content with a sandwich and a seat on the kerbstone, but has discovered that the extra gentility of a tablecloth and of service is within the compass of coppers after all, He may in his leisure half-day, and for no more than small silver, sit with the well-cashed exquisites of the city, may dine with music, and find himself included in courtesies as gilt-edged as the inaccessible guineas of a century ago. In this regard there is in Liverpool exclusion of neither cash nor class, and within a short radius of Clayton Square the restaurants are, for the combined characteristics of number, quality, and cheapness among the first in Europe. There is little doubt that in this socialising of the civilities of life, in the discipline of taste and refinement of habit which follow on the intercourse to which I refer, there is a revolution of habit which will reach beyond the mere mistaking of mistress and maid, of master and man. There has come a steepening of the standard, an irreducible addition to the universal demand, a multiplication of needs which speak with a more valid and invincible voice than all the demagogues from Thersites and Cleon to those of the present day. If the Soviet in truth pays for propaganda abroad, and would waken the workers to a feeling of what ought to be theirs, it would spend to better purpose and with more assurance of the issue, by investing to bankruptcy in the popular palaces of pleasure, by elaborating on the last elegancies of Clayton Square and of the places round about, by making a scholarship of the kitchen and an academics of the drawing room, and fitting both to a proletarian purse. The Soviet might then proceed to tie every tongue from Ramsay Macdonald's to Mr Wheatley's and Mr Cook's and having presented such a dining room as I have in mind to each town and village in the British Isles, leave it to speak in deafening tones for itself.

CHAPTER EIGHT

Chester

My road to Chester lay through Birkenhead, a town where every house is a last despairing addition to its neighbour, and every street a first turning on the left to something worse. For there is nothing in Birkenhead, nothing that is not a little further on, most of it so much further on that it is to be found in Liverpool. Its entrance is just an exit, its streets a slum succession of street corners, its main roads a mere medium for moving along them, and as for the shops they are simply places to spend the pence that have escaped the fate of pounds elsewhere. The citizens however are proud of their Park and their Square, places which are beautiful by the absence of what might be there, and which afford the visitor a view of the sky that he might in other districts not obtain. Indeed the unique charm of Birkenhead lies not in the buildings but in the spaces between, and this charm, which grows as one approaches the boundary of the town, may be enjoyed to the full in the fields beyond. And to this attraction might be added another which no-one neglects who visits the place, to wit the fine facilities for leaving it.

    I left it. Without a regret or even so much as a backward glance I entered the Great Western Station, which looked itself more like the dead end of a day's journey than the lively beginning of one. It was deserted and, as though not to be outdone by the town, it appeared as drab and dull as a drizzly dawn. I walked through its echoing emptiness to the booking office, took a ticket, though the assistant seemed to be wondering why, and as my steps tapped and tapped in the stillness to the train I continued to feel his following gaze. In fact there was no other gaze to relieve me of his. Did I see a porter? Possibly. Did I see an inspector? Perhaps. Did I see a passenger? Along the whole of my impersonal path and back again there was not a breath of one. Not a bag, not a voice, not a step but my own. For the stress of traffic and the press of people which I expected were, along with the lost and lamented loveliness of Birkenhead, on the other side of the Mersey. They had all gone into the world of Liverpool light, no further than a sparrow's flight perhaps, but gone, whilst I a bird of more permanent passage was winging the other way. I tramped along the draughty desolation of the platform and thought that but for the hard and deadened destiny of its being of stone it would itself have careered across. Even the lines which I could see glinting in the sunshine outside seemed to have wandered as bewildered waifs and strays into the wilderness of the station, to have blinded up against the last buffers in the wall, but still to grope like castaway ghosts on the Styx in longing for the further shore. So strong was the impression that on stepping into a carriage I recalled a verse which had been garbled from a Scottish gravestone, and which expressed the poorly plausible ambition that Liverpool might equal Rome. As cynicism it was sour enough, but there is a cynicism sourer still, against mankind be it said and not against a town. And the query is whether Rome will ever rival Birkenhead.

An hour later I was standing on the walls of Chester, a town which, as Rome, lives more by virtue of what it was than of what it is now, and one where the trace of the centuries and the track of the tourists lead to an idly idyllic illusion of both. For it is true of Chester, no less than of Rome, that fame has been so furthered by the fiction of it, truth so much by the trimmings, and attraction by talk, that only when things there are forgotten are they ever remembered. In Liverpool I was looking at life itself, in Chester I was meditating the mirror of it, piecing out the past in my own image, and affecting to see more in the darkling adumbrations of long ago than in the high noonday of the present age. I was back again in a waste-paper-basket world, and was pleased to amuse my imagination with the printed interest and parchment importance of former times, and to excite my curiosity by the scrap ends and crumpled oddments which others had been glad to cast aside. This might be irritating to a rigid reason: but is there any diversion more delightful than the antiquarian one of playing at blind man's buff with the bogies of what might have been, and of attempting in the mood of self-abandonment to count the waves on the ocean of surmise and to sort shadows in darkness? And are we to believe that such a practice is folly when all human wisdom hangs on the gossamer of a guess? when every hope and despair we have floats on the fading breath of a belief? when at any hour the dream may dissolve? and when with a puff the play may be over? And yet just as the future is a superstition of expectation, so the past is for the most part a superstition of print, a bandying of paper and of more paper with the lamentable lack of a dustbin as a fitting destination for the whole of it. We may flatter ourselves about the treasuries of remembrance but let us not forget that the past is less a leaf of life than a leaf of the book, a shibboleth of the library shelves where we number the nations as we number the pages, where we compress epochs into paragraphs, and centuries into ciphers. There is a Procrustes bed for it all, and thus with complacency we dare to pack personality into an epitaph, and only when the former is forgotten do we raise trophies to its memory, and only when the latter is obscure do we raise dust about the reading of it. And the requiescat in pace cries out in anguish from the ground.

After all I am no lover of junk, though some may ask what I mean by the word. Junk is an old word, but junk is a new one, and there is no syllable ancient or modern for which I entertain greater regard. It means much, infinitely more than it ought to mean, and it usurps a dominion of new meanings every day. Unburdened of its embroidery it would be in German 'plunder', and junk implies all that 'plunder*, implies and romantically more. We have other words, litter for example, and lumber is as good as any, but junk - ! I cannot help in this regard thinking of that trilogy of virtues, faith, hope, and charity, to which Paul in a passage of enthusiasm alludes. He eloquently enlarges on faith, he touches on the glories of hope, but the first and last fondling of his fancy, the unpriced pearl of his devotional choice is charity. Faith, hope, and charity, and the finest of these is charity. And so it is with the matter in hand. Litter, lumber, and junk, and the finest of all these is junk.

But despite the word I am no lover of junk itself. I have always thought that the dead should bury their dead, and should neither cumber the ground nor divide our interest for an hour beyond their allotted time. I admit it is otherwise with the world, for we are quaint amalgams of hope and despair, and are pledged by these, the first and final passions of the spirit, to the future and to the past. Although prophecy asks us to consider the birds of the air and the lilies of the field, to believe that sufficient unto the day is the evil thereof, there are few of us so reft of remembrance or so bare of aspiration as to live for the day alone. There is a hollow in the hearts of all for junk, and verily where the treasure should be, there will the trash be gathered together.

Now I said all, but perhaps I should allow a reservation, if for no other than Mr Ford, the millionaire maker of millions of cars. And why Mr Ford? Well, Mr Ford is a modern man, the most modern of modern men, with seemingly little time and less love for junk. Some time ago he took a trip to England, and among the sights he did, or was supposed to have done, was Oxford. Truth will have it that he is only supposed to have done it, but in fact Mr Ford did something better. He lent a further lustre to an already lustrous old legend, and gave it the climax that truth had long despaired of, and that romance had just as despairingly required. And the legend is this. When Mr Baedeker issued his first guide he angered many Englishmen by the following remark, 'Among the sights that must be seen are Oxford and Cambridge, but if time presses miss Cambridge.' So great was the chagrin of Cambridge, and so deep the disfavour into which the guide fell, that an alternative edition had to be issued where the remark was altered as follows. 'Among the sights that must be seen are Oxford and Cambridge, but if time presses miss Oxford.' Now Mr Ford in the dilemma of this advice did both. He did both, by missing both. He was not interested in old halls and colleges. Most modern as he is of all modern men he had no time for times that were gone. He paid no calls on the dead. He left no visiting cards on the tombstones. He possibly saw Oxford, a castaway glimpse of it, and careered on to Cowley hard by where there is a factory with thousands of employees, where there is business and bustle in plenty, and cash. The cordial clamour of the good people of Cowley, the discipline of their industry, and the prosperity with which that industry is repaid, so affected Mr Ford that, in reply, to an enquiring friend, he dictated a telegram as follows. 'Among the sights that must be seen is Cowley, and if time allows see Oxford and Cambridge. ' Yes, Mr Ford has his own standard of values, but none of these values is junk.

Naturally, Mr Ford, born and bred in a newer world, in a land that has neither history nor the air of it, would never dream of delving into the doings of the dead, nor would he ever, in any sort of senile sentimentality, bring up grey hairs in gladness again from the grave. He pretends to no marine-store emotions, no endearments of the dustbin, and is perhaps wiser than those who do. I had an instance of the wastrel unwisdom of the learned when in Chester, to which after these stray and straggling thoughts I return. I had wandered along the walls, stood on all the towers, and after coursing through the quaintly insetted arcades of the town, finally forgathered with the casually godly in the Cathedral. I had seen all, not all that the past had to offer, but all that the present had preserved, all the jealous illusions and hoarded idolatries which the faith of our fathers had cherished, and filial piety no less forborne. Yet as I entered the cloistered gravity of the Cathedral, which grew even more cloistered and grave in the fall of the evening, I felt in the tumult of the day's thoughts a hidden order, a still symbol of their society, a quittance of the crossings of criticism and of unrebated doubts, which in a tender dread of shadows boldly resign themselves to a deeper and utter darkness. I had come into the sanctuary, within touch of the secret and unrolled scroll of the law, within speech of the abiding principle which, personified at the altar and scheduled by science beyond it, is both the mystery and the meaning of all things. Here in the shrine itself, above the bolsters of belief and stays of tradition, clear of all the clouded questions of controversy, was the sign of the rule that ranges through the most aery and random relativities, the deified indication of the standard without which nature is unknowable and our knowledge nothing, the unsullied emblem of the measure, of the word, or of the number without which our wisdom had never been. This is what religion has revered, what philosophy has always sought and science ever applied, what each man equally gives and expects, what the babes and sucklings have unfailingly believed and fallible philosophers just as unfailingly failed to prove; the guarantee. For whether we accept God or reject Him, the quarrel is only in the license of a syllable, of no greater concern than the cuffings of the kites and of the crows, and in the grand career of things as forgettable. Nevertheless while the grain is growing in our own garden ground we are not happy till we have scoured the universe for the chaff.

Moreover whilst I was engaged in this thought I chanced on another of a true yet desponding character. As I sat in the Cathedral I suddenly recognised not only there but in all that I had seen during the day, in the crumbling gravestones outside, in the well-weathered walls of the town, in the half-tumbling and half-timbered houses of Watergate, in the fallen and fragmented Priory of St. John's, something more than a token of clinging kindred with what was gone, but a touch of the altar, an undying adumbration of animism or of the adoration of departed spirits, who having been before us were our originals in life, and who having proved of its pleasures and partaken of its bitterness, were our guides through it. In them, and in the memory of those we have loved and known is felt to be the last and safest instance of appeal, a reference which in hours of hard-driving dread and darkness, reaches above the ghostly guarantees of God and the eggshell assurances of science, and which, while making the past the pathetic arbiter of our hopes and bosom of our despairs, turns away from the pleasing aspirations of heaven to the sadder certainties of the grave. But the appeal is all one, whether to the love of our fathers, to the standards of science, or to the court of God. Certainty alone is what we seek, and disaster no less certain to receive it.

To me such thoughts are enough, but there are some, notably the learned among us, who are disturbed by details. As I sat in the hotel that evening ordering my thoughts by the play of the smoke and of the blazes in the firegrate, I fell into some talk with an elderly gentleman, a guest as I was and above all so sociable that whenever I applied the poker to the embers he responded and did a neighbourly turn with the tongs. He was a man of undoubted reading but of somewhat doubtful ideas, and as I gathered, a government inspector and archaeologist, who had come to study the antiquities of the town. He had been to the municipal offices, had consulted the town engineer, and sat there in front of the fire with the maps and plans spread out on his knees. I could see that he was in a long query with himself and I asked him why. He replied that there had been alterations to many of the remains, alterations which had weathered away into such a similarity with the rest that there was no telling which from which. "My difficulty, he continued, 'is that I cannot tell the good from the bad. I asked him whether by the word bad he meant what was old or what was new, and from that moment the tongs lay untouched for the remainder of the night. He seemingly put me down for a fool at once, and though I argued that if he as an expert could not tell the difference he had no cause to speak of good or bad, I appeared no wiser in his eyes. Clearly I was a fool and that was the end of it. And next day I saw him under his umbrella, shaking his head at the ruins, having come to the firm and irrefragable conclusion that half were good and half were bad, though which was which, and why, he had no idea. I think Mr Ford a much wiser man.

Somehow I had always thought toleration to be one of the graces of Academe, one who in Il Penseroso privacy held her court in the cloister, or more secret still in the studious and secluded school of the groves. But I find with advancing years that she is no less peasant than princely born, that she shows as handsome in homespun as in ermine, and that without loss of delicacy in the one sphere or of endurance in the other she can ply the pen and follow the plough with equal ease. After leaving the archaeologist I fell in with a simple man, a farm labourer and a natural gentleman, who knew Chester as simple people know it. I met him munching his sandwiches on the river bank not far from the bridge, and I am sure he would have been glad had I taken from his paper and eaten with him. As it was I sat down beside him on the grass while he talked of the town, which I suppose was never so interesting as when he found it interesting to a stranger. He knew Chester in the outline with which an idle eye sees it, and could tell me that the walls were old, very old, that the Rows were quaint, very quaint, and that the Cathedral was a building which all ought to go and see. Moreover there was a ruined Priory, St John's, perhaps I had heard of it, which learned men believed to be still older than the Cathedral, and should one care to walk a little further one came to this very River Dee which was pretty in summer when the boats were busy. And finally everyone knew of the racecourse, and naturally of this, when it was once mentioned, there was no end. Yet amid all the canterings of the horses, appraisement of the bookies, and deep old-world doubts as to the wisdom of it, he had still a word for Hawarden, the little village where he was born. I knew Hawarden? I didn't? Ah! that was something to see! Of course I had heard of the castle? and without waiting for my answer assured me that everyone had heard of that. Yes! Hawarden was an interesting place! Yes! Very interesting! and then added, 'If only for William Ewart Gladstone, our greatest man.' I think some cast of criticism must have come over my face as he said this, though I tried to be partial to his prejudice, and to bland over my persuasion that the fame of the one-time Liberal leader was only a twilight shadow of the fame that was. I wanted to be kind, for greatness goes the way of all gravestones, and even an eternal Old Mortality could never keep it engraved against the wind and weather of the world. I said I wanted to be kind but my friend was kinder. He saw my difficulty, saw that the now distant delight of his dream might be the nightmare of my own, rubbed his eyes to the realities, and said, 'Well, with Disraeli, one of our greatest!' The broad highway is certainly bright with the primroses of our unrepentant Spring, but were there no supporting sod of good intentions we might progress the whole way to the prodigal blazes with never so much as the glimpse of a bloom.

Since then I have had no thoughts of Chester without some of my companion on the riverbank, and my recollections revolve round him as did the old world of ideas round the apple of Eden. And this without a paradox. For what in heaven and earth is not built on the floating mote of a nonentity, and is there any wisdom that will not in time be draughted into the outer darkness like an autumn whirl of sybil's leaves? There is nothing in a cipher, and yet there is nothing in the universe that might not be lost in the hollow of it, and nothing in Chester that might not be lost in the least of its sons. It is thus that I have come to look upon the old city as one of very indulgent traditions, as a spot where time and tide are pleased to wait for man, and where they would even tarry for the dead if one desired it. I have but to recall it, and I am once again leaning a leisurely elbow on the Wall, by the Priory or maybe by the Bridge, or perhaps best of all overlooking the Cathedral, and am drifting in thought from the restless race of the present day to the standing stillness of time to a meditation of those dignities both of scene and of association, which have engaged the historian, inspired the poet, and enlivened the easel of the artist. Or I am once more in Watergate Street, lingering like a wistful wanderer of the woodcuts of long ago, and gazing at the vanity frontages of the half-timbered houses with their quaint gables and garnished casements, or pondering beneath the latticed loveliness of the oldest of them the text that God's Providence is mine Inheritance, and feeling that the future is in truth a promise of the past, and the past a no less pious pledge of futurity. Or yet again with a recollection of the name I am sitting amid the roofless ruins of the Priory, and making it a fable for those sentimental fancies which would see its weather-beaten beauty shadowed against the moonlit clouds, the wasted space of the windows and the arches obscured by creeper or by the bare branches of wind-driven trees, the high altar lying as in desolation under the omen of some solitary owl or passing raven. For though the winds possess it, though its secret has been uncovered to the sky and its sanctity to the storm, and though where once the shrine had stood is sombre with the brown of the autumn fall when spring is past and summer is splendid in the trees, it has still the illustrious loveliness of all the lost elegancies of long ago, the stateliness that is the due of adversity, the grace such as we see disclosed in a garland on the grave, or in the silvered glitter of the watery clouds after rain. For whereas here the tones of nature are blended with those of art, where the subdued greenery of life is mingled with the lively greyness of moss and ivy-grown relics of age, where the echoes of what is gone are in contrast and yet in harmony with ever-living voices, there comes a touch of time in the scene, a sense of the centuries, a re-animation of the past and a deepening of the present, that is found in no other landscapes but these. A presence fills their emptied peace, whispers of the fast-forgotten visitation, and the passing wanderer, who an hour before was surveying the hills and valleys as indifferently as the undulations of his own hand, enters here with a half-halting, half-tiptoe interest, or strangely sensible of the sounds, as of the solitude, pauses at some fence near by, and observes with a fine fascination even the fall of the least leaf or the soft hop of a bird. The familiar foot has indeed left the aisle, the speech has gone from the building, the stones have been delivered over as a trophy to the storm, but wasted by wind and weather they finally pass away into the Hand that sows by all waters, into the Hand that makes us the heirs of the green of the field, and returns us in death again to its dominion, that tempts us to the stars and treads us in the dust, and that, while bringing us down to a brotherhood with the beasts, elevates the least of these to that equality of life which makes of every insect a fellow citizen of the world and of every blade of grass a contemporary.

CHAPTER NINE

Stratford-on-Avon

It might be asked whether it is just a defect in my diary or rather a craze in my character that I have no admirations from which I do not dissent, and that any enthusiasm which I betray comes more from the feeling to be generous than from any intention of being just. I am apt to say yes to the first promptings of the spirit, but without loss of logic and moreover without scars of conscience, I could prove no to be a no less worthy answer. It is not due to my taste for dialectic, to the influence of the soul-fascinating sophistries of the schools, which I admit have their appeal. I should certainly not with any perverse bravado do a topsy-turvy stunt on the intellectual trapeze simply to show that it could be done. Nor is my nature any such conundrum that black has the possibility of being white in my conceit, but perhaps the reason is that from a criticism of others I have come to a contempt of self. Having a lively sense of my failings I am prepared to parade them to prevent their being paraded by others, and thus in constant anticipation of attack I am ready to reverse the role and lead the onset. It is a trait testified on every page of my diary and not a day passes without an appeal to the heart incurring a praemunire of the head, and without everything I feel being encamped against everything I have learned. And the anomalies multiply with the multiplication of my days.

Now I say this because here in Chester I was more astride the dilemma than ever, and whilst attracted to what are deemed to be attractions, and while falling into the devotions of others and giving the glory to both God and the guide-book, I no less believed that I was babbling to Baal. During the day I realised that I was on the wide Appian way of the world, and yet every evening I wrote in my diary that I had been travelling in the trail of my own illusions, and disposing my shadow for the bats and owls of unenlightened belief to mope in it. I might persuade myself in the ascetic close of some cathedral, or in the fragmented splendour of some fallen abbey, that I had an ear for the untouchable stateliness of things eternal, and an ear for the harmonic concords of the soul, but once beyond the precincts I saw everything enveloped in the brain vapours of superstition, curtained over with the cobwebs of gullibility, and appearing as some gigantic gimcrack which hobgoblins and jack o'lanterns might choose to joy over. Afterwards I was at pains to tell myself that I had been treading air, filling my belly with the east wind as Job has it, or pretending to a spiritual flight while performing no more than a clog fantastic on the cobblestones of egoism and conceit. Nor was there any difference when I turned to the industry of the towns. Here, admittedly, was much to interest, and distracted by the activity as well as inspired by the purpose of everyone around me, I felt that the labour by which we live was a better theme for reflection than the delusions in which we die. Even this interest however had its term, and wearied by the industrial dragonnade I began to indulge the old thought of the birds of the air and of the lilies of the field, and to wonder why the ungilded glories were so easy to have and yet so hard to attain.

A day later I was in Stratford-on-Avon, not the Stratford of story, where poetry has been pleased to figure the child of fancy 'warbling his native woodnotes wild' but the Stratford of guide-book clamour, the Stratford that begins and ends in a railway station, and which abandons the boosted banalities between to the charabanc and to the brawl of big business. I suppose there was a time when one might have spoken of the calm classicism and tranquil tones of our once perhaps most classic and tranquil stream the River Avon. There is even now when one looks from the bridge some discipline in its beauty, something superbly proper in the slenderly pencilled poplars on the bank, some sedate and symbolic air in the swans, some emphasis of piety in the demurely distant spire of Trinity Church. One has but to stroll by the riverside to come into quiet landscapes of elemental loveliness, to see, what in their simplicity most engage the eye and repose the spirit, such slight innocencies of scene as the common greenery of the field, the glinting gust of the wind over the waters, the rippled reflections of solitary trees. These are the nothings of nature, but when elegantly assembled as they are near Trinity Church have that expressive something which ennobles nature and art alike. There are eternal touches of it on the Thames, there are peeps of it on the unboated bends of the River Dee, and there are frequent and long glimpses of its forsaken fascination on the beatific banks of our manifold Avons, as in the southern seclusion of Amesbury, or in the spacious beyonds of Bath beneath Prospect Stile, or lastly in Stratford itself. It is a beauty that is not to be sought nor indeed to be described, but if anyone has an eye for these finer and more refined pleasures he may bury his book and still have read it, he may seek the solitude and still have society, he may spare the poet and still hear the solace of his song.

But it is nearly always an error to indulge the idle delight of a dream. A century ago Washington Irving wrote that when in Trinity Church he could think of nothing but Shakespeare, and that he could believe, in this persuasion that the spirit of the poet alone pervaded the spot, that the very stones were eloquent of his society - and as one supposes silent of God - and that even the graves lived again by his theatrical grace. There is such a thing as refining the feelings and distilling the thoughts, such a thing as spicing the platitude and candying the commonplace, such a thing as fondling the fallacies of those who are at peace in their own opinions and who will listen only to what they are pleased to hear. As for myself I saw Stratford Church in symbols of other things. To me there was a higher hope in the lofty and pleasing poise of the spire, a more religious richness in the meditative emblems of the windows, a deeper discipline in the dread of death amid the lengthening shadows of the graves than in the playhouse pieces of any poet, or in the mob admiration of his drummed-up memory. There are certain things which need no memorial, which live by virtue of themselves and of the mind to know them, and, were the tongues of men silent to-morrow, were every association erased from these walls, were big business bankrupt and Babylon and Bowry banished to whence they came, our Trinity Church would endure. For in the stately tracery of the windows, in the chaste and simple lines of the tower, and above all in the frailer grace of the spire is all the tutored dignity of English ecclesiastical art, an art so universal as to court neglect, an art that is no less original than its authors are unknown.

But though Stratford Church when viewed from the further bank still bears the precise and Benedictine spirit in which it was built, it has only an apparent privacy. There have been, in the lapse of time and of truth, coarse and cashy encroachments on its seclusion, a cast of commerce has come across it, a pall of publican profit, and the tuneful Te Deums which once resounded through the choir are now re-echoed in the till at the porch door. Moreover there is another building on the Avon, one in no very elegant keeping with the landscape, and which, coming as a garish contrast in the scene, has become a no less garish characteristic of it. It is the florid red Memorial Theatre, a building more blatant of the ambition than of the ability of the artist, an erection so American in its manufacture and so obtrusive in its appeal, that they who, like myself, have drifted behind with the retiring traditions of Trinity Church and of the Stratford that was, wonder whether a memorial is really meant and not an insolent and Sadducee assertion of the present day. One might still hear near Trinity Church despite the nabobs of New York and the shekels of Chicago, the 'warbling of native woodnotes wild' but here in a more modern neighbourhood is the caterwauling of backwood notes at their wildest, a tambourine oratorio of vanderbilt voices, a hurdy-gurdy ecstasy in up-to-date tammany taste and Rocky Mountain refinement. There are indeed some ironies of landscape which, in their gravity of contrast or in their heaviness of humiliation, we are the more pleased to indulge, and which incline us to those contemplations of human nature and of human destiny which find only a sadness in disgrace and a dignity in adversity. For instance when in Rome we are not disturbed on seeing the squalor of the present quartered on the splendour of the past, nor have we any emotion but that of interest when in spots which history has exalted and poetry embellished the mob follow their own motley amusement, and all unmindful of their former glory and of the manifold memorials of their once mighty empire, parade their paper pageants amid the columns of the Caesars. Nor have we any other wonder but at the stillness of the scene and at the strife in our thoughts when we come across some ancient castle that still stands in all its tumbledown desolation of battered ambition and abated pride, and we see the cattle quietly grazing in the shadow, the sheep nibbling amid the mouldering stones, the peasant baiting his horse in the moat at the wayside. But these are the diversities of destiny, incidents of the universal fable where each feels something of the fallen fortune of his humanity, and traces a likeness in the travail of his own lonely soul There may be a contrast in the scenes themselves but no comparison, and where no comparison is pretended no caricature is implied. But the distance from Trinity Church to the Memorial Theatre is the distance of travesty, the tawdry distance of pretension and pretence, a step to such international and niggerdriven devotions that all who indulge in them are convinced that in crying up the common taste they are best commending their own. And like the Pharisees, under the pretext of giving the glory to God, pocket the compliment of doing so for themselves.

    Whilst at Stratford I was not forgetful of my pensum which was to pace the broad highway, to photograph what was expected to be photographed, and to observe what others had thought worthy of note and description. Shakespeare's birthplace was in my round, and my only eagerness for going there was to correct an impression of two years ago. In those days I had a camera insufficient for my purpose, small and without adjustments, and on reaching the house I perceived that a photograph was a problem of some difficulty. The building I decided was very indiscreetly placed, and to add to the indiscretions of the site numbers of motor-cars blocked the approaches on either side. A front view was the only possibility, but try as I would I could not include the house in my finder. If I tilted my camera to secure the roof I failed to get the floor, and if I tilted it back to recover the floor the roof disappeared from view. If I turned to the left to get one side the right vanished, and if I turned to the right the left slipped entirely out of the picture. I had no choice but to retreat, and by a freak of providence, or of the reverse of it, a huge swing gate yielded behind me and I backed into a yard. The roof indeed appeared at last, but not until the gates and the cobble-stoned entry had so grown on the picture as to fill all the foreground and to usurp the whole interest of the scene. At this moment I backed into the arms of the proprietor who seemed indignant at my invading his place and photographing his backdoors without leave. He was one of those men who are proof against the amenities of immortality, and fail to be flattered when less honour is accorded to the front of Shakes-speare's house than to the back of their own, one of those who prefer private right to public recognition, and seclusion to celebrity. So I withdrew; but though his personality may perish, his possessions, or rather the gate to them, will endure, for my picture, crude as it may be in conception and still cruder in execution, is nevertheless a privileged piece. It is an allegory, in which is to be seen the preponderance of the present over the past, of the commonplace over the elect, of the things of earth over the fictions of the spirit. And, as one can see, the gateway to both is very much of the world.

I took my second picture of Shakespeare's house in a more favourable and less inspired hour. I had come to Stratford on the day of the celebrations, a yearly festival, which might for the ease of visitors be removed to the Mississippi, and in which all who have never read Shakespeare make a pleasing penance by pretending that they have. They are a fashionable host, who, in the thin intervals of races and regattas, jazz and the social jungle, are induced, perhaps as much to impress themselves as their friends, to fondle an affectation for letters in the public street. For just as there are many who suave over their solecisms, their upstart syntax and gutter grammar, in a refined pronunciation, so there are many more who by a bank-holiday enthusiasm - not for art but for the inartistic advertisement of it - and by bumpkin applause - not for the artist, but for trite and town-crier talk about him - hope to clamour themselves up as cavaliers of the muses. To such minds fashion and the numbers indulging it are the heaviest persuasions, and that these persuasions might not be wanting in weight all the ambassadors of the nations, especially of those who have least heard of Shakespeare and, in the press of better things, never will, appear in the procession, meeting at least for once in unanimity, though whether from courtesy, conviction, or ignorance, I for the same motives but the last shall refrain from deciding. But in their presence one might naturally affect to believe that the voice of the people is the voice of God, and if God's voice in this disguise has more barrel-organ bathos than piety expects or faith allows, still faith and piety will always agree that the almighty tones are less to be understood than to be heard. And in Stratford they are content to hear, for however fervent the festival and however colossal the crowds, the sale of the tales of Edgar Wallace is not affected.

I am afraid that my only feeling when in Stratford was that of the Athenian citizen who voted for the exile of Aristides as he was weary of hearing him called 'The Just'. It was not said in envy of Aristides, nor in criticism of his character, but in a well-seasoned cynicism of those to whom hearsay is evidence and popularity the proof of it. Moreover to identify anyone with the first of social virtues is either to blaspheme the virtue or to flatter the man, bringing the one into contempt and the other into caricature. Doubtless the Athenian citizen must have felt that not only personal happiness but social salvation was the issue, and, because it was easier to banish Aristides than the populace, banished Aristides. With more claims to justice though less to practicability I should banish the populace, and should not flinch from making a desert and calling it peace, even though the peace were my egoist own. Yet if it were only considered that the merit we each have is the measure of all we delight to honour, the desert and the peace would come of themselves.

CHAPTER TEN

Leamington and Warwick

There can be few who have left Stratford with so little regret and with such happy expectations of other parts. I boast of much local emotion, a feeling which admits not only the associations but the place itself to our esteem, and which according to Johnson it would be no less impossible than foolish to set aside. But though I have this feeling, and in no small measure, I am pleased to temper it to my prejudice, and am prone to slight a spot as I slight the celebrity in whose name it became famous. Naturally if local emotion is to be approved, local bias is not wholly without reason. There are too many who believe that fame is the best proof that it was deserved, and who in this belief trust for the value they buy to the price they pay. This is certainly a simplicity that saddens with time, for no innocence however stubborn will bear up against a big progression of bills. Between the follies of finance however and the fashions of letters there is this difference, that while the former yield to a poverty of the purse the latter triumph in a poverty of the spirit, a deficiency which being in our days the less despised is the longer endured. For sympathy is not the least of our virtues.

I left for Leamington by bus, a conveyance which in comparison with the train discloses more of the countryside and casts one more among the people, but which by its discomforts makes one indifferent to the interests of either. In the freshness of the first few minutes I saw Charlecote House, parked in at a secluded distance from the roadway, and caught a glimpse of the deer, which in their frailty of form and timidity of disposition, accorded as well with the feudal expanse as with the cultured char-acter of the park. It was a landscape of estated dignity such as we see everywhere in these parts, and which, even if history had not added its interest and poetry its associations, would still have that full appeal which the minstrelsy of Middle England has so idyllically expressed and romance no less idyllically confirmed. Beyond Charlecote however I was engaged not with thoughts of the journey but with desires for its conclusion, and failed in my impatience to observe Warwick or to preserve any other impressions than that we left it behind. It is probable that Leamington, tasteful and attractive as it is, never looked so agreeable to a traveller's eye as it did to mine when I alighted on the Parade.

Though I have my prodigalities, praise is not one of them, and yet to Leamington I give the word agreeable in all fulness. Our ideas of England are so attended with trade and industry, with tumultuous thoughts of London, as well as with the smoke-blackened prospect of the north that it is difficult to conceive of a truly English town where smoke is anathema and where tumult is taboo, and where labour is less known than the leisure which should follow it. But such is Leamington, or to be accurate, without being either ironical or complimental, Leamington Spa. We say Spa, but in Central Europe they say Bad, a distinction which many have coveted and multitudes acquired, and which is apparently now bestowed on any place which may have air to breathe or water to bathe in. But in England Spa is not a title so universal as to give distinction to those without it, but is an honourable addition which you would share with

Leamington alone. Not Harrogate in all its upland aloofness, nor Bath in its terraced historicity of tone can claim such a style, which answers so well to the light and leisured agreeableness of Leamington, to the propriety of its buildings, and to the elegance of its gardens, and which, while promoting the pride of the people, preserves them from the unrefinement of other parts.

As Jephson's Gardens were hard by I went in, paying a small fee at the gate. I have never paid a fee with less reluctance, for though only a penny it perfected its purpose. It was small enough to be given without question, and large enough to prohibit any abuse of the park. My experience at Buxton was different, for I am not one of the well-cashed exquisites who can say good-bye to silver without emotion. I remember going to the garden gates there and debating long with my canny self, alternately consulting my conscience and inspecting my purse, for I was professionally bound to take a picture. But the spirit of parsimony prevailed. I stood on a seat in the roadway overlooking the park, and took a photograph from there, having demonstrated in this one gesture my business sense as an Englishman, my reputation as a proletarian, and my character as a guest. But at Leamington I was saved from such a shift as this, and for the poverty of a penny was afforded perhaps the most pleasing gardening prospect in Europe. I say pleasing, for naturally I shall not measure its charms against those of Versailles which is of infinite ambition, as well as of greater age and of more ordered design. But one word is needful lest, to the mistake of such a comparison, we add the grosser one of injustice. English gardening is free in its interpretation of landscape beauty, and seeks without precision of pattern and without regularity of arrangement to combine the wildness of nature with the cultured graces of parks. Though the lawns are well rolled and the paths primly kept there is caprice in the position of the trees, in the scattered flower-beds, and in the occasional and evergreen plantations. He that has been used to the town, to the rectangular rows of the streets, to the geometric alternations of doors and windows and tiers of bricks and stone, turns with the pleasure of relaxation to the refreshing freedom of the trees and flowers of an English park.

It may sound perversion to some, a squibbish opinion which it is wit to express and wisdom to abandon, but I could see a thousand Stratfords in ashes in return for a Jephson's Gardens in every town of the country. In fact were Rome on the Thames I should say a thousand Romes, and for a reason. A pilgrimage to any place of celebrity is like a journey to a fountain. However we go, whether on foot or in a chaise, we carry away no more than our bucket will hold. To go therefore to Rome with a vacant mind as most of us do, is like going to a well with empty hands. What we gain by the dinning advertisement of these places, by the new miracle of the wilderness, whereby we change the scarce caviar of the scholar into a cartload at cod for the tourist crowd, is not easy to discover. Its effect is surely to debase taste and to deceive the understanding, for what is lovely only in allusion and sacred in association becomes ugliness when the allusion is lost and the association is unknown. But in Jephson's Gardens, whether we look along the elegant license of its variegated avenues or survey the church from the rose-rambled arbours beyond the lawn, or ponder the well-plumed poplars so superbly suspended above their rippled portraiture in the pond we find a dainty diversity of scene, a fine and felicitous play of prospect, to please every eye and to amuse every mind. But how can I describe what can only be known when seen? Some weeks later meeting a friend who had returned from England, I asked him had he been to Leamington. He had. He had seen Jephson's Gardens? Of course! And his opinion? And here his face assumed an expression of appreciation which was more ample than any reply. Indeed words fail to describe what my friend failed to describe, and therefore I shall endeavour in the interests of truth to fail to describe it. This alone I shall say: that he has nothing of nature or of cultivation who has just a scant glance for such graces as these, for an art that is as excellent as it is English, an art in which we were once unique and are still now without a rival.

It was whilst idling by the pond in Jephson's Gardens, with the drums and tramplings of Stratford still in my ear. that I indulged some very old thoughts which have the air of heresy in these days. They were thoughts of natural beauty, and I wondered why it was that both the Alps and the park before me, though so opposite in their aspect, were alike beautiful. I wondered furthermore whether, if taste were altered, we might stem the tide of holiday-makers overseas, or perhaps, were such gardens as I have mentioned more general than at present, balance the loss by visitors from abroad. It is possibly a hardy statement, for which I have no proof and for which I can argue only my impression, when I say that most of those who go a-broad do so, less with the idea of seeing other lands than with the idea of proclaiming the fact on their return. They do not go for languages in which they are little skilled, they do not go for ideas of which they are entirely destitute, nor do they go for architecture and art seeing they are so gracelessly ignorant of the treasuries of such at home. I see little that is elevating and much to lament in these stampeding droves of trippers who are brought into the penetralia of foreign parts, as the old barbarians were introduced into the arcana of Christianity, converted in hordes and baptised in battalions. Advantageous as foreign travel may be, it can become a wasteful evil when it degenerates into logging up the places, notching notabilities, slaying kilometres, and sandbagging the time. People who do these things are not wandering, not freely wandering at their own wistful wills amid scenes which recall those at home only by contrast. They are marching and they are marching to a tune. Moreover they are marching to a manufactured tune, to the sounding brass of the American Express Company, to the banging of the big drum by Thomas Cook & Co. Big business is the conductor of the band, and it is a very big band. There are no solo parts. It is one great organised American grand extravaganza from beginning to end. There was a passing parallel in Japan some time ago. The ancient city of Kyoto was elaborately decorated for the enthronement of the emperor. All those who could, assembled at that one spot. They numbered five millions. At the dramatic moment the prime minister led a solemn chant. This was taken up by the assembly three times, till the song culminated in one deafening shout from those five million throats, one universal, hyena, halleluiah howl from five million heads, each as empty of sense as the howl itself. That is the demand. Noise. It is the rout of reason. It is something which deadens one to every other thought. But there are other thoughts and these may be pondered in silence. And this silence I found, first in Jephson's Gardens, and later on in Warwick Park.

It is only a short walk from Leamington to Warwick, and from the pictures which I had seen in the shop-windows on the Parade, as well as from the descriptions of people I met, I began to think that anticipation might even be the least of Warwick's delights. In the first hour, however, I grew more tolerant to such travellers as prefer foreign parts. I might stroll along the Banbury Road to the bridge, and there amid the dust and smells of the traffic-ridden highway look over the Avon towards the Castle, but to take a more privileged and private view from the river, or to ramble along the banks, which are as certainly the heritage of an Englishman as the air above them, was barred. Surely a litter of houses that add nothing to the beauty of the spot and much to the vexation of the visitor might, without loss to the pocket or to the reputation of the nation, be littered elsewhere. To afford pleasure to the traveller is to bring profit to the town, but to talk of trespass, a language which ought in such places to be spared except to those who utter it, to flout popular expectation and to make proclamations of petty right on the broad pathway of public interest, is the surest way to speed our people abroad, and to empty the expense of their pleasures on foreign soil. What poorer boast can a nation have than beauty unseen? What sourer solace than delights hoarded and never enjoyed? What more beggarly prospect than the face of a bond to its possessor while the debtor is comforting his innards with the spending of it? The places which nature has ennobled, which history has honoured and art adorned, are common keepsakes, which to our personal pride and to universal emulation ought to be maintained against local slovenliness and national neglect. They are what is first sought by the stranger and longest remembered, and such impressions as he obtains determine in no small measure our standing abroad. But how shall he respect what we refuse to respect ourselves?

Before entering the Castle I took a stroll to Leycester's Hospital, not a hospital in our sense, but in the older meaning of a place of hospitality. Looking down the road one might take it for a church, which in the drift of devotion had hovered over into the highway, and had been patiently propped up by the faithful. The support however is no other than the old West Gate. Here was the portcullis and here the defending tower, but Leycester's Hospital is the ancient row to the right. It has its name from Leicester, the favourite of Queen Elizabeth, who in a moment of piety, a feeling to which he was little prone and for which he was never famous, devoted these buildings to the maintenance of twelve poor brethren and their wives. The foundation is still extant, there are still twelve poor brethren, they still amble through life in the blessedness of their wives, giving God the glory daily, and on Sundays magnifying Him by magnifying themselves in the quaint hats and robes of the days of Elizabeth. The buildings are equally picturesque, Old English and half-timbered, embellished with the coats of arms and with the heraldic devices of noble families that have contributed to the Hospital. The courtyard is interesting, the banqueting hall distinguished, and poor though the Brethren be they have an opulence that passes economic understanding. I spoke to one of them who seemed at peace with the world and still more so with the beyonds of it, but who had no spiritual gifts except the happy impression that he produced. He had well survived the flames of youth, and was now superior both to poverty on the one hand

and to philosophy on the other. His pipe was an absolution from all troublous thoughts, his tobacco a sufficient viaticum to serener scenes, and with every pleasure narrowed into the breviary of the glowing bowl he appeared to find the sole industry of his retiring days in the salvation of a spark and in the stricken perdition of many, many matches. After some talk with him I discovered also that his yea was yea and that his nay was nay, but what was more than these was more than he could vouch for. So with a tip I bade him good-bye. Verily pence, however humble, are a salve to many sorrows.

Ten minutes later as I paid my two shillings to enter Warwick Castle I thought of him again, and reflected how much comfort to him might lie within the compass of those two coins, how much repining at expense in my own spirit, I have always been a little elegiac about my L. S. D., but the dirges which I indulge are less on what I lose than on the ease with which others earn it. If anyone however were to insinuate that my feelings had more of envy than of equity I should perhaps be staggered for an answer. But enough of that. My two shillings had gone, an admission ticket was mine, and its value was what I should make of it.

CHAPTER ELEVEN

Warwick Castle with certain thoughts on Art

Picturesque as parts of Warwick are, there is nothing in it more picturesque than the castle round which it has grown. Like the town it reveals in itself an array of the ages. The deeply parkland approach, the gravelled drive and the trees are naturally the additions of later and more elegant times when the unruly barons had disappeared, when the perils of invasion had passed, and when the nobility had turned to peaceful arts and to prosperous pursuits. The towers however, the embattlements and the barbican recall an obscurer period, and though time has taken away their terrors, and though the encroaching greenery has softened the severities of the scene, they still bespeak the barbarity of the builders, and in even greater degree the intrepid passions of the warriors against whom they were erected. Yet with all its might Warwick has not the character of the fighting fortresses of Wales, of those steep and stupendous strongholds, which, hewn out of the grim granite of the hills, stand out bleak and bare against the buffetings and the brawl of the Atlantic storms. The impression at Warwick is more of present peace than of past brutality, of culture than of conflict, of the antiquarian than of antiquity. There is no menace in the towers, no omen in the long shadows which they throw on the green. The postman as he enters the battlements bids you a rural good-morning, the baker's boy cycles up the walk, the gardener idly sweeps the fallen leaves from the grass. The barbican, emptied of its perils, scarcely returns the echo of a footfall, the courtyard betrays no other presence than that of the traveller himself, the residence, modestly handsome amid the veiling ivy, reflects from its windows nothing but the sunlit solitude of the lawn. The wanderer who comes with the perilous expectations which history has induced and fancy animated looks only on the elegance of what the centuries have spared, sees the minor but ennobling niceties of a cultured landscape in little, and forgets all else in the well-appointed prettiness of the demesne. If he is wise he will labour no illusions, and will silently leave all his former thoughts amid the dust of those who inspired them, and if piety finds an expression in his being he will hope that the souls which so enlivened his imaginings are in as delicate keeping as the castle by which they are remembered. For if the work of our hands may endure, who will not trust that the final travail of the spirit may also be preserved?

By chance I fell into some talk with a gardener, who, without slighting the house for which, as I discovered, his reverence was less of knowledge than of habit, prevailed on me to view the Park first. The suggestion was doubtfully put, and for many minutes he rigmaroled between his hearsay enthusiasm of the Castle and his informed admiration of the Park, but at last his pride triumphed. 'Yes everyone enters the apartments, but-, ' and as he cast a querulous glance at some trippers coming up the drive I knew it was a distinction to have an understanding for the grounds. Of all the vanities that of a gardener is the most forgivable, for praises of him are indirectly the praises of providence, a tribute not only to ability but to the bounty which rewards it, a due both to a utility and to a beauty as lasting as time, and no less universal than nature itself.

Agreeable to the suggestion of the gardener I went into the Park and was at once afforded a glimpse of England as she still is in favoured parts, an England of aristocratic walks, of stately trees, and of patrician stretches of level lawn. There is landscape in the elegant and gracious gardens of Middle England, perhaps nowhere more elegant and nowhere more gracious than in Warwick itself, where water and woodland, field and foliage, lofty trees and still loftier towers are blended into prospects of peculiar beauty. There is naturally neither perfection in the pattern nor discipline in the design, but even where diversity passes into licence there is refinement and grace. It was whilst I was standing on the long walk looking back towards the Castle, which lay distantly obscured in the retrospective quietude and ordered tranquillity of its own afforested domain, that I recalled my thoughts on natural beauty, and faced by the handsome aspect of the Park I compared it with the scenery of Wales, Scotland, and the Alps, and began to wonder why I had ever considered them fine. I have a sense for symmetry, a passion for form. I never write without rhythm, without pondering and playing with the balance of syllables and sounds. I am nothing if not musical. I admire a measure in all things. And yet I have stood before the Alps in all their rugged and broken-down barbarity, a tumbled riot of rock and snow, and have spoken of their beauty. It was in Warwick Park that I asked myself had I been talking truth, if I had not been adding my voice to the general eruption of tourist rant, if I had not been hustled by the travelling agencies, if my genuine judgment had not been bludgeoned by the flattening platitudes of the press. By every standard of art, and every one would appear to demand exactness of contour, equality of line, evenness and refinement of form, the Alps in all their gross and gruesome ugliness stand condemned. They may be attractive, they may ease the city-tired eye, they may uplift the spirit, but beautiful they never were. They were never thought so two hundred years ago, and I wondered why we think so now.

This may appear an unhallowed heresy to many, a lamentable lapse into a philosophy of long ago. But I must distinguish. I have two grievances, one, a big one, against Big Business, and in this most would concur, and the second against 'love of nature,' where I may count on disagreement. While standing on the drive with a distant glimpse of Guy's Tower in the background I was reminded of the verse which is both the catechism and the condemnation of the Romantic Age, - 'That every prospect pleases and only man is vile.' It appeared to me to be a gross untruth. As I looked on the ordered freedom and lightly disciplined elegance of the walks, trees, and lawns of Warwick Park, a park as cultured in conception and as dignified in the intimations of unobtruded art as any gallery piece, I stifled that superstition in myself for evermore. Beauty begins not with nature but with man, as much from the elaboration of his hand as from the choice of his eye. The thought that nature is pure and that man is vile, that there is something divine in the powers around us, something devilish within ourselves is one of the rabid errors of the romantic poets. Shouted from the housetops of Geneva it found a too ready echo in the cellars of London and Paris. It infected politics and became embalmed in much preservative verse. Apparently there was a divine ordinance in things, and only in man was divinity and ordinance missing. The poet began to pose as a prophet and a preacher, and to ministrate in the amiable mysteries of the natural world. There arose a cult of the gossamers of life, a holy communion of the commonplace, and, intimidated as much by this talk as by the absence of a head and tail to it, everybody made a great kow-tow to the Alps But the spring is taken out of every year, its fragance passes, and however beautiful and brave the blossom may be, it must someday be littered in the wind. There is night as well as day in nature, the winter's ice as the summer's warmth, sadness as well as joy. The sun is not always standing at noon, and man, about whom the universe is only noddingly mindful, is lost at last amid the lengthening shadows of declining life. Indeed with the coming of the evil days as adumbrated by Ecclesiastes comes also a feeling of kinship with them, a passing of pleasure and a failure of desire, with no hope and no expectation of a break in the deepening clouds that return after rain. We have the fate of the flowers of the field, the sad destiny of the lesser celandine, which tenderly hides her early blooms at the first touch of the tempest, but later when the bloom is gone helplessly submits her buffeted beauty to the bluster of the storm. It was perhaps a vanity of primeval virtue to speak of death and decay as the wages of sin, whereby we were happily confirmed in humility and contented in humiliation, and were pleased as tributaries to nature to accept the afflictions of age as a hard assurance of the justice of God. With such dark and secret equity we might even when old have time for the eternities, and might, when ideals were buried and ambition on the pyre, still favour ourselves with a hope and find the end no despair. But the void of the world is not to be filled with desires, nor its silence with the answered anticipations of humanity, and they have the surer though harder belief who see in the order of nature and not in the option of man that the days and the years are numbered, that only a child carries childhood to the grave, and that the portion of both vice and virtue is the dust.

On my return to the Castle I saw the gardener once more. He seemed pleased with my compliance, and as I rang the bell of the house I answered his pleasure with a courtesy which was as much an honour to his opinion as a homage to his art. I was only a tripper, but doubtless I am among the few who have entered the apartments of Warwick Castle without a following frown. I was certainly received without one, and was conducted through the rooms with a courtesy, which one expects but rarely experiences, by a most efficient guide, one who invited enquiry, one who spared neither information to questions asked nor time to interest displayed. But thoughts of the gardener kept obtruding themselves, and I fell into comparisons which despite the ability and politeness of my guide impaired my pleasure in both. After all the gardener could vary his flowers, could add a cubit to the stature of his trees, could dispose of the prospect by winding the walks and displacing the waters, and however great the ravages of fire and time would think no loss beyond repair. But my guide of the castle might speak of history but could never reproduce it: he could not touch the tapestries without damage; nor add a dot to the Van Dycks without disaster. Perhaps it does little credit to my criticism to have thought so, and no honour to my justice to have indulged the comparison. Yet I noted the fact in my diary to explain why I saw so much and observed so little, and why amid so many curiosities of art and so many felicitous illustrations of long ago I bore away no more than the burden of my own ego, but - under the weight of it - the wish to lose it, and the still further wish to see Warwick Castle again.

    Unforgettable however were the portraits, not only for the personalities depicted but for the talent displayed, a talent which bespoke an age when art implied the skill of the artist and not simply the acumen of the critic, when the painter was pleased to paint and the spectator still more pleased to appreciate, and when explanation was required only by fools in front of masterpieces or by the wise in front of daubs. I have always thought that a craftsman is one who leads you into his confidence, not one who lumps you into your own confusion as had been my fate a few days before in the exhibition of modern art at Liverpool. I had wandered into the gallery and had drifted through a room or two, when either my aimless attitude which was very apparent, or my grilling glances which were more so, drew the attention of an artist whom I had known before the war. He was at that time a man of simple life, and as simple in the expression of it, a man for whom the circumference of a sixpence comprised many joys and at times even a margin for luxury. Life had really an embroidery in those days. One could be nobody and there was still room. But that, as I said, was before the war, and the time had now come when there was room only for his own understanding and with it a defiance of the understanding of everybody else. He showed me his picture. He saw my perplexity, and to help me out of it he talked of a colour scheme, emphasised his value point and elaborated on arbitrary focus. These were just the technicalities, handmaids to a philosophy which he be800000000000000000000000belaboured to my broadening embarrassment. He was aspiring, he said, to a personal view, to an insight into the psyche of things, and he paused for a word from me. 'Well, ' I replied, 'it may be philosophy, it may be psychology, it may be technique, it may be each of these things, it may be some of these things, it may indeed be all of these things, but one thing it isn't, it isn't art. ' He was good-humoured, and offering his hand by way of goodbye he remarked, that only on two beings could the spirit make no impression, on the stupid and on the realists. So we shook hands, and went our several ways, I with my stupidity - and with my realism, and he, simply, with his stupidity.

Though art lies in concealing art, it is sometimes obliged to assert itself and conceal the subject. But not even Holbein, with every flattery of the brush, and with every artistic sleight of hand that fear might prompt or profit prescribe, could veil the bucolic abundance of Henry the Eighth. As was natural Holbein did not venture to add anything of his own, while, on the other hand, to lessen the portrait would be to prove, perhaps impolitely, that there was too much in the sitter. It was Burns who implored the gods to give, what they have always had the wisdom to withhold, the power to see ourselves as others see us, but Burns might have known that this was the finality of all afflictions. Holbein might have known this as well, and though he afforded to Henry the power which the gods failed to bestow, he was perhaps aware that Henry, like his memory, was of the stuff that endures. Indeed truth has its triumphs no less than art, and the portrait, whatever the intentions of Holbein and whatever the expectations of Henry, appears to confirm what history admits and posterity believes. In the unbeatific bulk of the body and flaccid fattiness of the cheeks, in the insensate space of face, in the peevish lips as well as in the hard unliving eyes we see Henry as his deeds declare him, a pampered footpad, the coarsest clod of unchristian clay that ever publicly confessed the crimes of others in order to be privately absolved of his own. Yet he who could run through a fortune, six wives, all the monasteries of England, and the faith of his fathers to boot, was no common man. We are willing to think so after seeing another portrait which persuades us to softer opinions of Henry, and to a gentler judgment of his blood-besodden career. It is a portrait of a child, of Henry himself, and in the innocency of his early features appear those trails of glory which are first boasted when finally abandoned. But who cares for the excellencies which come of grace and not of gain? It is with men as with books. Only antiquarians, men with fanaticism and the money to maintain it, have a joy in first editions. The world demands, and persists in having, the last unexpurgated copy. The baby portrait speaks indeed with the tongues of angels, but the world has decided against Henry, and the final picture of Holbein pleads trumpet-tongued against the deep damnation of its deciding any differently.

There are other pictures however in Warwick Castle of a more designing delicacy and of a still more flattering finish than the unposed non-possumus of Holbein, and of these the most distinguished both for what it reserves as for what it reveals is the portrait by Van Dyck of Charles the First. I might never have guessed the uncommon skill of the artist, his criticism of character even on canvas, his fastidious poising of the problem how to tell truth and rule our reception of it, his artful communication of emotions more native to himself than to his client, had I not seen another picture of Charles in the National Portrait Gallery of Scotland. Now I had never thought hardly of Charles, for I had read

Clarendon before looking at Carlyle, and whilst a revolutionary in all other spheres I was, even to my own surprise a royalist in the cause of the Stuarts, There must be few families in history, who to so much eminence have added so much mystery as this one, and there must be fewer still about whom controversy has said so much and decided so little. Throughout the whole of their saddened story, and especially from the misfortunes of Mary to the plight of the Pretender, there may have been deeper tragedies than that of Charles, but he above all others made some show of innocence, and furthermore, that he endured imprisonment without reproach and met death without a tremor are facts which have given his name to romance and ransomed his memory from the disrespect of his enemies. The picture however in the Scottish Gallery put an end to all my pietist opinions about Charles, and induced in me a readier admiration of the higher honour and erecter character of the Hampdens, the Pyms, the Miltons, and the Cromwell who struck him down. In no single feature does he recall his father, who is very pleasingly portrayed in the same gallery, and who to traits of distinction and a look of scholarship adds a quaint cast of discouragement, a glance of miscarried enquiry which helped me to believe of loftier hopes, of better ambitions, and of more dignified ideals than history allows him. Certainly the historians have been more open-minded to Charles and no less open to question, who if the Scottish picture is any guide, was as ill-favoured as the derelict Anne of Denmark herself and had the expression, and maybe some of the character of a faceless fraud. And yet Van Dyck, without any of the finer infringements of veracity which the nature of art demands, which vanity naturally expects and flattery of necessity concedes, has from a farrago of feeble features painted a face which wins the word handsome from hosts of observers. The straggling length of figure, so disagreeable in the Scottish portrait, has gone and a pyramidal pose, attained as much by the delicately outstretched hands as by the distending of the dress, imparts a pleasing balance and adds a stateliness of demeanour, which is at once the deceit and the design of the artist. An engaging melancholy hides the emptiness of the eyes, a kingly elegance disguises the general negligence of expression, while the sallow length of the face, happily emphasised by the descending collar and the succeeding star, conceals by a contrasted obscurity the unshapely nose, the ignoble lips, as well as the unmanly narrowness of the chin. And how much refinement of purpose lies in the flow of the hair, obliterating the stoop, breaking in on the effeminate expanse of the collar, and informing the face with a rectitude which the nature of Charles never knew, and which no act in his career ever confirmed! The Eikon Basilike was thought later to be his most eminent memorial, but there is a more majestic image of the king in the felicitous fictions of Van Dyck, who whilst he refused with exact artistry to paint the vanity of a sitter was able on portraying a thing of earth to breathe into it as much the air of superiority as the breath of life.

The simulations of the gallery were in such agreeable keeping with the semblances of the Castle that I was persuaded to every reflection but such as the past naturally inspires. Here was the countenance but not the character of antiquity, and I found myself idling in the drawing-room shows and shadows of sedater times, mistaking rather than making the acquaintance of that ghostly company of vanished faces and of defaulting voices, which the piety of posterity, no less than the hand of the artist, has retrieved from the grave. The daylight world was beyond the windows, but none of its animation entered this tranquil cabinet of illustrated life and of pencilled personality, the tapestried story and engraved anecdote of which were to be contemplated at the academic leisure of the observer. With such impressions I might have described Warwick Castle as a memorial without a remembrance, rather a present courtesy to the past than an ancient heritage to our own day, had I not seen that perfection of portraits, the picture of the doomed Earl of Strafford by Van Dyck. There was passion in the brush that painted it, that passion which is the first condition of skill no less than the final consummation of art. At a glance I saw that this was not the Strafford of the artist, but the Strafford of history, the hard adventurer who diced for the honours which might have been his by right, who, born to be the buttress of a kingdom, died the bauble of a king. The despairs of stricken greatness are usually not without dignity, nor are they ever without those reserves of resolution which temper the exultation of enemies and which abate the grief of friends. But the despairs of this finely pointed and inspirited face are not of death. The crumpled collar, the dishevelled hair, the set lips, the half-reflective half-impassioned frown, above all the levelling look of the eyes have indeed something of dread, but it is the dread of dishonour not of dissolution, of a disgrace that no courage could defy and no defiance could absolve. Here was a man who began with popular applause, a man of such pre-eminence of spirit, as to make his opinion the earliest enquiry of the Parliament as well as its ultimate decision, who as he 'disposed of his yea and nay' disposed of the faithful yeas and nays of the country at large, who was as foremost in affronting power as he was later relentless in quelling discontent, and whose abilities, when he entered the royal service, 'made the prince rather afraid than ashamed in the greatest affairs of state. ' That he bargained with ambition might be forgiven him, that he was abrupt and overbearing in prosperity might also be defended though not denied, and that he defeated his own deserts by courting favour rather than by seeking fame had revenges of which he lived long enough to be aware. But that such a face, where every feature reveals the directness of decision and the ascendancy of character behind it, should have been subservient to the face of Charles, and should have thought homage to such an infirmity an honour to itself, is an offence against the spirit which, as in a symbol, anticipated the block by many seasons. He had his judgment. Even the severities he exercised were less than he suffered, and if he betrayed his party he had the bitterness of being betrayed in turn. He who had little to hope from the mercy of disinterested enemies could expect nothing from the vengeance of offended friends. The canvas has certainly been kind, and Van Dyck, perhaps more than in the case of Charles, has proved his advocacy, but no tears are eternal. Every tomorrow has a duller ear for yesterday, and however loud our lives may be in word and deed or in the acclamation inspired, they have not the validity of a whisper in the emptiness of a vanished world. Looking at the portraits in Warwick Castle I felt that these also had voices in their own day, voices which the birds of the air bore abroad, and to which every wind wafted an answer, but voices nevertheless which are echoing away into the secret confessional of time, while the spirit which moved them has passed on into the absolution of all things.

CHAPTER TWELVE

Kenilworth

From Warwick I went to Kenilworth, going by way of Guy's Cliffe. I did not keep to the main road, but took a long circuit over the fields till I came to a spot from which I could see the house beyond the mere. The place where I stood was enclosed with trees and occupied by an old mill that was said to have Saxon associations. These I was willing to believe, as the aspect was pretty, and the construction, though recent, quaint enough to be older. I took a photograph, which I flattered myself was superior to professional efforts, as the season was early and the trees bare of the foliage which in summer stifles the view and curtains out glimpses of the sky. I had thought that I was confronted by a lake, but the waters were those of the Avon which had just escaped from the weir where the mill stood, and which flowed past Guy's Cliffe situated on the further bank. The scene has its own sufficiencies, and requires neither legend to enhance its interest nor poetry to preserve it, but traditions, though for the most part as fleeting as air, are in such spots as enduring as the sunshine and the rain. Guy of Warwick has vanished from history, but he survives in romance and continues to spend his aged days in the solitude and austerity of the old wooded estate, while the good Lady Phyllis like the Penelope of Homer's story awaits the return of her Lord. Mythical figures of course, and they have had their passage; but they still linger on as the frail and faded leaves that float on the delaying waves of the River Avon.

The house has not the air of Guy's story, nor even of a relation many times removed. But just as there are generations of men so there are generations of buildings, and this is of the eighteenth century, ample and baronial in style, but more expressive of the opulence of those by whom it is owned, than of the skill of him by whom it was built. I remarked to an artist who was seated on the wall sketching the view that the beauties of the house were rather of position than of plan. He agreed, and then to my surprise added, 'And believe me every stone of it is touched with the blood of a negro!' I had heard the sentence before, for it was a reproach against Liverpool flung by an actor at a hostile audience there, but the artist assured me that his expression was independent - as is to be hoped was his information. He explained that the original wealth of Guy's Cliffe was the wealth of the West Indies, and that without the oppression of the plantations and the sadness of slavery it might never have been. I was disturbed by these remarks, as I had found it easy when looking over the drifting ripples of the Avon at the feudal aloofness of the house and the trees, to think of Guy of Warwick, and to persuade myself into the ballad beliefs and into the well-rhythmed unrealities of long ago. But to me this story of the eighteenth century lay still deeper in legend, nor could I inform my imagination with symbols of the time when every shadow of Guy's Cliffe was more sombre by the dark story of transportation and of lingering exile, and when every bush bloomed with uprooted beauties from afar. It is a prophetic utterance to take no thought of the morrow as enough for the day is the evil thereof, yet we might with better assurance of content take no thought of our yesterdays. The sins of the fathers verily descend unto the third and fourth generation, but we are happier when spared the knowledge of it. So I turned to the artist and after commending his sketch which was a bad one, and then consoling him for his grievance which was even worse, I went on my way to Kenilworth.

There are two Kenilworths, the town and the castle, of which the latter is in ruins, and the former unfortunately in repair. Indeed if ever proof were needed that all human felicity has its date, but that the poor are always with us, Kenilworth would supply it, for here the only beauty is the boast of a beauty long since departed, and its only prosperity the proclamation of the decay of it. The rest is an illustration of the demand of Aristotle that every work of art must have a beginning, a middle and an end, though it might be suggested that Kenilworth has no end of all three. There is certainly no end to the main road which is a long-drawn-out agony column of grocer grace and of chandler charm, devoted to the traffic of small change and to the tragedy of cheese-paring profit. But these are the tears of things. The smells of them, as testified by the fish-shop fragrance and supper-bar ozone, as well as in the other burdens of the provincial breeze, are of a higher nature, and reveal in proportion to their elevation the base degrees by which they did ascend. Instead of loitering as I had expected amid the old-world loneliness of an historic Kenilworth I found myself scuttling before the unarcadian gale, convinced that wherever Scott drew the facts for his romance the atmosphere must have been his own. Perhaps the silks and ermines were, with which his poetical fancy invested the Kenilworth of history, or is it that we now see her in the sackcloth and ashes of her dowager days, resigned to the distresses of indigence and to the regrets of recollection? It is with towns, I suppose, as with men. It is fortunate for some people that their fathers were born before them. Their paternity is their capital, the piety of the believing world their income, and their only task in the sinecure of celebrity is to keep the epitaphs in repair. But even this task is a trouble to many, who are pleased to abandon it to the pride, or to exact it from the purse of others, and still more pleased to allow themselves all the applause.

My first misfortune in Kenilworth was to see it first, and my second was to fall in with an American whose airy ignorance of anything historical and whose lightness of literature took the temper out of all my contemplations of the castle. I am not despising him. It was rather his place with his abrupt and breezy practicability to despise me, and I should have resigned myself to any ridicule had he not been on the same errand as myself. I met him buying films for his camera, and the shopkeeper, thinking that the American had money to spare, offered him something else. The American refused it with the plain observation that he would not buy what he did not want, and then to avoid any two meanings on the subject asked him again for what he required. He was not rude, he only wanted films, and he received them. We went out together, but before we reached the door I knew his name, learned where he was going as we stepped outside, and before arriving at the castle I had gathered as much of his personal history as I should confess of mine after the intimacies of years. He made no mysteries of anything nor curtained his character behind any of the common courtesies. With his hands in his pockets he shouted his enquiries to the policemen across the street, accepted all answers as a matter of course, and passed his free and easy observation in all openness to those we met without either impoliteness on his part or embarrassment on mine. There was the usual rout of card-sellers, photographers, and drivers of touring cars at the gate, but he strode through them all, blandly oblivious to their appeals, and finally entered the grounds with the assurance of a man who had paid his fee and who was not to be bluffed of any part of his bargain.

As far as history went his information was of the flimsiest. He had an open and prairie space of mind with no obscurantist corners for the crickets and cobwebs of twilight erudition. He knew of Elizabeth. She was a queen. He had heard of Sir Walter Scott, - a man who had written many volumes. But on my speaking of Leicester he cut me short, telling me with a wisdom I admired, that he did not know him. By this he meant in person, and therefore I could spare myself any description. Seemingly what was beyond proof or at least beyond the pale of his experience was superstition, the proper place of which was the obscurity where it prospered. We strolled over the green and entered the banqueting hall of which I instanced the history, but he was less curious as to how it came into ruins, as astounded that it had never been repaired, and he wondered why we should labour at the resurrection of walls which were thought not worth the saving grace of a roof. Not a name I mentioned moved him to a closer enquiry save that of Cromwell. I related that the castle was given to Parliamentary officers who made no better use of the gift than to strip the roof, rifle the apartments, and knock down the collections to the highest bidders. 'Quite,' he rejoined, 'they could not use it themselves?' No! 'Nor could they find a buyer for the whole?' No! 'So they sold it in lots?' Yes! and he was surprised that I had expected them to do anything else with it. I could not quarrel with these observations, for my companion was not one of those who came with a rustic admiration of what he did not understand. He did not come with a gaping mouth and swallow everything, nor with widely saucered eyes and see nothing. He had his views, but he was not to be flunkeyed into others because they chanced to be commonly expressed, nor was he tempted to abandon his own at finding them universally disapproved. In view of his independence I was interested in learning whether his distaste of Scott was from ignorance or conviction. He had read little but had found that the best way to read Scott was to miss the major portion altogether. It is a common criticism and a just one. Certainly it is the only criticism likely to disturb the Waverley empire, which though dispossessed of its ultramontane might of a century ago is still a superstition with us, but no more than a superstition. Scott no longer divides with Napoleon the interest of humanity. Though faithfully bought he is, save for Ivanhoe and the Heart of Midlothian, as reverently shelved. We have promoted him from the pocket to the bookcase, honoured him with the deep and undisturbed retirement of a leather binding, and said masses for his literary soul by looking to his appearances in the library. My American friend however would not have allowed him tie obsequies of a bookcase. 'I see no sense in studying the characters of men who are dead, nor in reading descriptions of things that no longer exist. ' And in this I think I agree with him.

My interest, for all that, had been so engaged by the infamy of Leicester and by the afflictions of Amy Robsart that, but for my friend, I might never have observed that there is a Kenilworth of fact as well as a Kenilworth of fiction. This was natural, for just as when reading we seek rather the romances of Scott than the history of

England so the eye is attracted by Leicester's buildings and overlooks the sterner testimonies of a ruder age. Amid more amiable meditations the Norman Keep had escaped my notice but not that of my friend. He had sauntered with a certain indifference through the great hall but had now found something which invited his interest and added to his understanding. Here indeed were none of the artistries of the residence, none of the frailer felicities of style, which even when crumbling into ruin, persuade the fancy to thoughts as frail and as felicitous, and which partake in their nature of the fables wherewith we are pleased to involve them. Here the gravity of aspect proclaimed the simplicity of purpose, that of battle, to give blows and to take them, to inspire assurance in the defenders, to strike terror into the hearts of the enemy. So it has stood for seven hundred years, a bloody and impregnable blockhouse, bearing the brunt of heavy civil strife, and surviving the rapacities of peace even more triumphantly than the ravages of war. This is what Cromwell failed to destroy, and while the sumptuous additions of a more elegant age are hastening to the ground, this bastion of baronial ambition remains. Reminiscent of romance as Leicester's buildings are, handsome in age and graceful in decay, they leave no such abiding impression as this grim Norman Keep, the story of which is perhaps all the more provoking in interest as it is a story that has been left half-told. My American friend, whose forward but rather rough judgment quietly gained on my esteem, was for photographing the Keep. Whilst approving of the plan, I remarked that a picture of the banqueting hall would be more than a mere addition to his album. He was of another mind however and shook his head. Such windows could be seen anywhere, and though ruins were rare in his experience he was glad of the fact. I tried to obtrude the word picturesque, whereupon he rejoined that were the former owners to return, and see what time and plunder had effected, they would find the word picturesque somewhat misapplied. The buildings might have been beautiful once, but to think that charms were added, when the roof was stripped off, the windows broken and the interior laid waste, was some impressionist fad which was more an honour to my imagination than to my understanding. I thought of Scott, and illustrated again the associations, but I was strewing my old-fashioned seed by the wayside of the New World, and finding myself with only an empty bag and a following of crows for all my pains. Why should he photograph Mervyn's Tower where Amy Robsart, whom he did not know and in whom he was not interested, happened never to have been? 'If I am to follow fictions like these, ' he continued, 'I had better begin with my own, buy postcards of places I have never visited and concoct conversations with men I have never met. The only pictures I shall take are those which have quickened my curiosity and which will serve to confirm my accounts when I return. ' I asked him, perhaps not without irony, if that was a part of his pleasure to talk about his travels when back in the States. 'A part?' he asked in surprise, 'It is the whole!' If I had undertaken this journey under the condemnation of being dumb about it, I should have been in agony for the rest of my days. ' He then cut me short by telling me that his camera was set, and begging me to press the trigger when he was in position. He posed very impressively in front of the old stronghold, and I hope he was pleased with the result.

My friend was not without his influence, for though my first impression of Kenilworth was the Kenilworth of Sir Walter Scott, my last and certainly most enduring one was of the Norman Tower. I left it with such reflections as are shadowed by the dissolution of ages of endeavour, by such feelings as arc further darkened by the adumbration of our own derelict destiny, and I came into a catchpenny confusion of poverty booths and public-house humilities which reassured me of the justice of mortality. Time has dealt harder with Kenilworth than with Warwick, which is still calmly mirrored in the answering serenity of the River Avon, and which still commands the courtly acres and pleasant prospects of Warwick Park. But here the contrast of present desolation with former splendour, between the terrors that were and the trivialities that now are, gives to Kenilworth a cast of calamity that we seek for at Warwick in vain. Its closely islanded seclusion has gone, and the lordly lake which in the days of Elizabeth afforded the elegant pleasures of the barge, the civilities of the moonlit masque, and the tuneful solace of the madrigal and the lute, has, since the marauding times of the Protector, been drained away. The moat has been emptied, the woodlands felled, the park ploughed over, and now the rustics and the townsfolk roam at will over what was once one of the proudest domains of the land. These hobnailed intimacies are indeed no humiliation, but there are ironies still more roughly shod, which tripping over modern lips, bruise the heel of departing greatness. As we came out of the gate and cast our eyes on the pothouse prospect beyond, my American friend turned to me and said, 'Well it is queer, you can afford sixpence to preserve ruins and not a penny to improve realities.' I remarked that the preservation was no loss as the banqueting hall might always serve as an example. 'Yes,' he replied, 'and these pubs as the efficacy of it.' Whereupon we parted, he to Coventry and I back to Leamington Spa.

CHAPTER THIRTEEN

Oxford

Next morning I decided for Oxford but not without misgiving. My visit was to be just an American-tripper peep into the library of Oxford life, no more than a fluttered review of the headlines, whence I might guess the text beneath and suppose to myself the pleasure of its perusal. There are some who have a taste and some a talent for these dilettante diversions, and who think that the contents-page and the index dispense them from the pons asinorum of the book. Perhaps nowadays when most books are an unnecessary comment on the tides, when it is the function of professors rather to prove their own importance than to instruct their students, and when almost every volume is another dusty and dunciad addition to the pedantic pile, such taste and such talent are less to be condemned than applauded. As with study so with travel. Often a name is enough, and what a glance fails to include, imagination easily supplies. Yet for all that I confess that I have little joy in these swift and swallow flights over the surface, catching the gnats of knowledge and the flies of information, while the angler who has both the time and the tide at his disposal bags much bigger and much better game. Sometimes I pretend to have seen the world, but my pretence is no more than the hop of a hedge sparrow through the harvest, and my ambition no higher than to boast a spot somewhere under the eaves of the barn. It is the best that the best of us may hope for, so that when I was at

Oxford I was content with what a glimpse from the highway could afford me.

Of the university I shall not presume to speak. A seat of learning is not to. be judged from an inspection of the buildings, just as no man's character is to be concluded from the cut of his clothes. Carlyle with something of a cynical glance at the academies of his day said that the best university was a library, and assumed, what he in his cynicism would scarcely have allowed, common sense in the use of it. But I shall leave the remark to its own refutation. The only university worthy the name is the society of better men. In the depth of their intimacy is the degree of all education. This is moreover a commonplace of the schools, for after all what are books supposed to be but the gathered thoughts of those who know more than ourselves? and what is the lecture room but the chance of hearing one who speaks with authority? In both cases however, in the library and in the lecture room, intimacy is missing, the corrective contact, the personal spur and inspiration which, in the privacies of the spirit, is always the beginning of better things. The fast friendship of one remarkable man, and we shall not meet more than one, is value for all the fees we ever pay. He may be a professor, he may be a student, he may, and it is not excluded, be even the porter at the door, no matter: if he is a personality, if he is one who can think in feeling and feel in thought without being unprecise in either, and if he gives us the privilege and the inner hospitality of himself, we are in the best university on earth. Mutual understanding is the one and only condition of education.

Such a thought excuses me the folly of national comparisons, as like causes operate equally in like conditions. Still in a Continental mind there are superstitions about our universities, and such fables of sport and pleasure are popular as common sense should query and a visit serve to obliterate. That our education is no dragonnade is admitted. We certainly carry our academic crosses very cavalierly and with a rather easygoing grace, and few Englishmen, I imagine would go gruelling themselves to the grave for the sake of an examination. But to assume that our universities are a round of endymion delights, that education is a plaything of taste, and a degree the reward of residence, is a fiction that can only gain credence among those whose vanity of greater effort is not to be shamed by their vexation at no better success. The Hill of Difficulty is as steep in England as elsewhere, in my private and unsupported opinion steeper, but there are reasons why it should appear to be otherwise. The Germans for instance are in very pathetic earnest about their universities, their homage to higher education is, with the possible exception of Scotland, unequalled in Europe, and prostration is the only proper gesture to a professor. In England academic celebrity is, like a Sunday morning sermon, something to be slumbered over. Indeed I read in a review some time ago an article deploring the attitude of Oxford students to the staff. Apparently to a superciliousness of opinion they added a slighting languor of speech, above all in reference to their studies, and numbers found amusement in proving their professors to be just so many noodles. Whether healthy or not, it certainly skittles the pundits from the Salisbury spires of impossible pride whereon they are sometimes pleased to perch themselves, and it quite as certainly saves the student before his examination much nightmare mopping of his brow.

As my visit chanced to be during the vacation I was surprised on walking down High Street to see so many students. They were hatless as was to be expected, and with sporting jackets as evidence of their earnestness and bags as no small part of their importance, they appeared to confirm what foreigners are only too prone to believe. They had none of the distractions of study in their glances and none of the ardours of athleticism, and their hands were, without exception, lost in the Bohemian idleness of their pockets. Inquiry, however, revealed what a closer acquaintance verified, that these young men were not of the university, and though all had the cut of students none had the credentials of study, a combination which often makes distinction difficult. Seemingly everyone in Oxford is ambitious of a studious appearance, and in this regard many effect more by the purchase of pants than others by the belabouring of their brains. Be that as it may, they one and all attain a degree, and no student pretends to more, of make-believe, for it will be found on reflection that titles are necessary only in a world where they are unjustly bestowed.

Social distinctions however must be maintained. They who have more pretence than proof of superiority find solace in appearances, and make up by a lavish elegance of dress for their lamentable lack of desert. Where virtues are vague, fashion is obvious. If it stampedes into extravagance as at Oxford, and borders on the absurd, I am inclined to look less to a straining of taste on the part of the crowd than to a despair of distinction on the part of the elect, and to see a vanity ultimatum by the students to the multitude of their imitators in the city. Let the student in a perspiring pursuit of singularity sport his plus fours, and every crossing sweeper will sport his expansions in turn; let a student have his bags and the pants of every errand boy will have the sack. But no evil is without its alleviations. Historians who flatter us on the growing refinement of manners will rejoice at the softer civilities of Oxford, and will note that the blood and thunder strifes of town and gown have been liquidated in the milk and water emulation of town and trousers. Instead of suppressing an enemy with bludgeons they now impress him with breeches, and hang all the laws of elegance and all the prophets of propriety, as well as the upper ten commandments of caste, aristocracy, and academic exclusion on belts and pairs of braces. Even the old idolatries are outdone, and from the affectation of the golden calf, we have come by plus fours and the short skirt to an exhibition of the human one, who—without any Trinitarian subtlety— is the biggest of the three displayed. But progress brings its abatements. How fortunate that we rely on the ancient oxen for the name of the city and not on the modern calves for its reputation! and who will conceal his chagrin at the decline from the roast beef of Old England to the half-baked veal of our own day? Reading Genesis I observe that Jacob above the bounty of men-servants and of maid-servants rejoiced more abundantly in his many camels and in his many asses. It is a wealth that is nowadays unknown but it is a spectacle that we still have to be spared.

As I strolled along High Street I had to admit a disappointment. From the old woodcuts I had learned to think of a reserved and rural highway, one which divided the more retiring interests of the artist and of the historian and where each might seek attraction or instruction, and find it. My impressions were of an Oxford that is gone. Prepossessed by my reading of long ago I was anticipating the idle and dominie air of the ancient engravings, and had expected amid the old drift of the stiller civilities of college life, to cross a rustic or two, to see an occasional carriage and pair, or perhaps to tread a little incidental grass between the cobbles. Even what was uncouth I was prepared to contemplate as the graces of age, and had believed that the frontages however oddly defaced would appear more venerable, the sculpture though quaintly crumbling more picturesque, the quadrangles more academic in their vacational tranquillity. To these illusions of character I added more amiable ones of construction. In the old-world drawings of High Street which I used to linger over, the bends had been pleasingly emphasised, and while the single spires of Magdalen, or of St. Mary's, or of All Saints were allowed to excel the scene, the further felicities were engagingly contracted to a glimpse or as engagingly excluded. The distant towers were involved in the foliage of protruding trees, cast in dimly architectured shadows, or lost in brave sweeps of descending cloud. Indeed I had so indulged these elegant economies of equivocating artists as not only to perceive in each building the beauty of its own presence but also to entertain the expectation of beauties beyond. With every view I entered into the hidden distance of things, and have left myself in happy suspenses in tracing out the forms which time has obliterated, or have trifled away hours in the graver vanities of divination in speculating on the purpose and fate of the curious and roughly sketched figures and on the forgotten wonder of their forgotten ways. But these are the faded and late afternoon fancies of the study, vagaries from which reality rudely recalls us, and to which we return only in such indulgences of twilight dreams as delight the recluse. They are visions which boast neither a breath nor the society of a shadow, and which a touch of the day will dissipate, visions which, while betraying little of the past, and divulging even less of the future, serve only to reveal us to ourselves.

A century ago High Street was thought to be the first thoroughfare in Europe, and had - what is rare in a town of such antiquity as Oxford - a width that added dignity to every edifice, and what is more a length that allowed to the eminences of style a diversity unequalled anywhere. Scanted of its greenery as it now is, disfigured by posts, and distracted by traffic, it has little distinction save those of associations, which the buildings can hardly display, nor the interest of the traveller well discover. In the fuming speed of the charabancs, motor cars, and tractors which course through it, all thoughts of antiquity are thronged out of the mind, nor have thoughts of art better access. The variety of view which the graceful curvature of the street once afforded, the contrasts which were thus agreeably accented, the comparisons which were thereby artistically evoked, are better believed than seen. There are things that only the eye of a disciple discloses, nor does the faith of every pilgrim keep step with his feet It may be a melancholy admission but I number myself among those who in the modesty of their mortality make no attempt to remove mountains. Perhaps when Baedeker takes precedence over experience and belief over both, the former enthusiasms may again be indulged in the High Street of Oxford. Meanwhile I shall reserve mine for the century-old and millennially elegant illustrations of long-forgotten folios, and shall resign all my recollections of the common racing track to such as made it so.

The interest of Oxford is to be tempered only by the taste of the traveller, limited only as his time, and bounded only as his opportunities for inspecting it. Many students would affirm that this interest begins and ends with the river, and would even venture to say that Oxford as a university would be in liquidation without it. Indeed in the belief that its banks contain the capital element for floating companies and colleges, watering intellectual credit, and sinking paternal funds, some are tempted to let study drift, and to sponge as much on the reputation of their alma mater as on the finances of their sires. Wisdom of course is not to be purchased, but where a sale is there will the fools be gathered together. They who expect something for nothing, knowledge without enquiry, scholarship without solicitude, and talent without toil have certainly the bliss of expectation. The folly of being wise is a bitterness that they are mercifully spared.

 I reserved the Thames for Sunday morning, and strolled along to the picturesque spot where the Cherwell, flowing between lines of poplars, joins the river. It was a very still and sabbath scene, for there were few people about, and the only break in the ecclesiastical gravity of the landscape was my uncanonical camera and my secular self. The impression was pleasing but I improved on it as I returned towards Folly Bridge. Quite by chance I came to a view even more vacational, one familiar neither to the student nor to the visitor, to whom perhaps such idle interludes between the tumult of the terms present no attractions. At this spot the trees were happily arched and through a break between them I caught a glimpse of a church spire. Pagan though I am, and almost pious in my apostacy, I was not proof against the saintly spell of the scene, and as I photographed it I gave it a habitation and a name, the holiest of Oxford habitations as I have heard, and the most honoured of names. I called it 'A distant prospect of Christ Church. ' Whether the Thames at Oxford has any fairer views to offer I do not know, as I was interrupted by an old man in a punt who thought I wanted to cross. He was polite, but I eyed him with a little doubt and inwardly multiplied his motives since the Bridge was not far away. Was he a contriving old fellow cornering me for a consideration, or just a simple soul desirous, in the simplicity of both spirit and understanding, of doing me a service? It was a problem where to secure truth was not to serve justice. I might refuse his offer and whilst eluding his duplicity offend his innocence, or I might accept and by withholding the tip confound his guile and yet defraud his virtue. There was the problem, and the fate of both, my pence and my pride hung in the balance till he spoke to me again. 'Of course, ' he said, 'you will be too early for the service. ' Burdened as I was with a camera and a field glass I allowed him simplicity, and when stepping out displayed my own by giving him a silver piece which he had not the wherewithal to change.

While strolling back along the wooded walk towards the Meadow Buildings I was reminded of Bonn. The trees are not so stately, the paths more confined, but the Hof Garden would naturally be lost in the meadowed magnitude of Christ Church, and Bonn lacks what Christ Church enjoys, an unimpeded prospect towards the river. Still the scholastic setting of the Broad Walk, the long lines of elms, and the unblushing parade of youth, beauty and fashion, or as much of it as Oxford can muster, made reminiscence easy. I did not seek sanctuary in the Cathedral which I had seen, and which, while presenting many points to be noted, possesses none to be renewed. It is said to be the smallest in England, and I trust I am not unduly intruding myself when I say that it is the least impressive. It is of every age and of every style, and has been all that a place of worship can expect to be or hope to experience. Wolsey found it a church and left it a chapel, and Henry found it a chapel and reformed it to a cathedral. In appearance it is an array of afterthoughts, being a quaint combination of Norman simplicity and of later decoration, picturesque in parts but discordant in design. Moreover there is little of that devotional air which we look for in a church of such antiquity, and which in smoothing out the incongruities might have attuned the mind to a more contemplative inspection. So little was I affected that when approached by the verger I secreted my guide and left my simplicity to his discretion. He discovered more than I confessed, though little in proportion to what I concealed. And when we parted we did so with a respect which mutual ignorance alone inspires and which separation can alone preserve.

Really architecture is one of the good-humoured affectations of travel in which, by private whim and by public wink, words are allowed to fulfil the office of understanding. He who knows nothing may, by the pretence of name and by the nimbus of meanings, assume an amiable omniscience, and may persuade himself into an appreciation of art, and others into a respect for his attainments. Problems that have taken centuries to elucidate are comprehended in a glance or dismissed with the nod of superior knowledge, and technicalities that would pucker the brow of a craftsman are lumped under the common of-courses of conversation. Indeed it will be found that those whose subtlety with blocks of granite is surpassed only by their simplicity with packs of cards are able to sum up everything but themselves in one word: interesting. Yes, 'interesting' is the word: everything is interesting, and if anyone is at a loss for comment, especially if he is uncertain as to which object is being shown, or is perplexed by the explanation, or is ignorant of its significance, let him remember that the phrase 'That's interesting' covers a multitude of misunderstandings, a phrase so versatile as to include thanks to the guide, a tribute to the artist, esteem for his handiwork, and above all a tip to one's own intelligence and good taste.

This curtness has another virtue, that it saves us from multiplying words without wisdom and noise without knowledge. Once we emancipate the tongue we enslave the ear, and though we may wave the white flag of weariness to our tormentors the red rag of rant continues to flap in the breeze. If the tongue is to be our ambassador, as it needs must be, then let it be an ambassador in bonds, not a plenipotentiary accompanied by the provocation of drums and trumpets, but a brief and private envoy, one who ensures peace by preserving it himself. And when shall the world know such a peace, that Utopian peace where the tongues shall cease from troubling and the talkers be at rest? As yet the world knows only a two-minutes' silence in memory of the dead; when shall it enjoy a two-years' silence in oblivion of the living? Verily the prophetic voice cries nowhere but in the wilderness, either in the wilderness of other voices or in the solitude of its own, and is never heard. Even the echo of it has long since died away in the rush of the east wind. Ages ago, in the days of the Tower of Babel, God wrought confusion on mankind simply by disrupting their speech whereas nowadays He makes confusion worse confounded by leaving the language and allowing us to understand.

Perhaps the worst that can befall wisdom is not to be neglected, nor even to be misunderstood, but to be most honoured when fools presume to explain it. Only to God is it given to survive the glosses of the godly, whilst His prophets are left to the fate of being famous and of being known by the pandemonium of their apostles. Indeed it is the tragedy of so much truth to be interred under talk, and of so much art to be consigned to the ungodly God's acre of comment, that I am in dread of adding by any words of mine to the vain and valedictory dust that at last drifts over all things. I am content if truth delivers its own testimony, prophecy its own fulfilment, and beauty its own applause, and further am content to believe that if any splendour endures it will be for its due and not for its adulation. Flattery after all is best left to epitaphs, where it is most easily forgiven and least remembered, and where the bones can offer no disproof of their praise. Here even cynicism may dispense a tear in sadness if not in sympathy, and may, in a gasp of gallantry, allow a little licence to the last clamours of the grave. For they awake no echoes in the cosmos, nor do the drums of death and the tramp-lings of darkness dun the universe to our belief, nor make of the answering silence an assent to our persuasions. But fame is a feverish thing, and when in life we have failed to utter the prophetic word to our fellows we fly to the funereal wordiness of friends. For who is pleased to believe that the earth will forget him, that the universe will leave him unnumbered in its memories, and that he and all that was his have been wasted in the world.

CHAPTER FOURTEEN

Along the towing path to Reading

My way lay along the Thames to Iffley, and I kept faithfully to the towing path which leads through the fields. I had idling ideas of Iffley, shreds of the reading and of the reveries of distant days, when I had learned of an old mill and of a still older church, and had thought of them ever since as coverted in the quietude and forgetful-ness of the river. Of Iffley village I had, and perhaps willingly, more vanishing fancies, a farmhouse or two faintly seen and all but lost in the shadowed deeps of the evening, and an odd countryman whose dim and retiring figure added an air of 'the day is over and the harvest home. ' I am jealous of such early illusions, and they with a responsive jealousy never leave me, but float lightly on as thistledown through life, drifting from day to day and from dream to dream and escaping all the brambles and thickets and branches of my worldly way. To these illusions I add moreover the pastoral affectation of poetry, and though a treader of towns, and both in body and spirit eternally stumbling over the cobble-stones of my back-street existence, I am still an architect of aerial Arcadias, still a king - without the commission of a kingdom, an idling idealist on the dole - and still idealising. Let reality be what it will I shall never omit to mingle imagination and memory, nor deny myself the indulgencies of those dreams to which even the towing path yields a tribute and even Iffley inspiration. But it is one thing to see Iffley with the mind and another with the eye, and half an hour later after leaving Oxford I was standing on a road that led seemingly to nowhere, not even to Iffley, and there before me was a lonely trio of buildings, a post-office, a school, and a church; a post-office where stamps, halfpence, potatoes, and village humanity foregathered in communion or in a silent mass, a school where the innocents of both knowledge and iniquity were taught the will to remember and the wisdom to forget, and a church where the denizens of that post-office and of that school were buried in hope, wedded in delusion, and baptised in despair. An old church with an outworn philosophy, but could I 'exchange the bells in its belfry for the bats in my own, and ring my spirit back to the old reassurances, I should gladly confess a further infancy at the font and as gladly support the charge of second childhood. Yes, life is a lonely thing and Iffley an emphasis of it.

As Iffley was without appeal I sought once more the reticences of the river and the rustication of the towing path. Here I should surely escape the sing-song of civilisation, and eschew the high sessions of the Old Adam who is most at home when abroad with friends. April has its privacies on the banks of the Thames and showers of rain give a happy assurance of solitude. Moreover till Nuneham Courtenay there is little to attract others and less to distract oneself, and the wanderer may without disturbance pursue the tenour of his way and the tenuity of his thoughts, and leisurely leave the destination of both to time. My only burden was that of the path, which is ill-kept in these parts, unkempt, overgrown with rushes, and interrupted by marshy tracts, and my toils through the wet grass and the mire allowed me no contemplation of anything else save the gray vacancy of the sky and the flat unpastured expanse of the fields. I passed Kennington Island and should have liked to cross over to the Swan Inn which lay in castaway tranquillity under the ragged shadows of the trees, but the ferryman was away nor was there any passing oarsman who might have taken me over. The house itself looked very deserted in the leaden light of the morning, nor did I see any smoke from the chimney, any face at the window, nor hear even the bark of an abandoned dog to prove there was more hospitality in the Swan than the empty offer of it. But the promise was plain enough on the notice-board - luncheons, teas, and finally an added etcetera which rankled my curiosity and edged my disappointment. Possibly it is an error to garnish expectations and to relish regrets, but I still meditate in dreamland and after-dinner hours on that etcetera, and wonder why that which was refused by fate has become endeared by time. What never was will always be esteemed above what is. Indeed just as the most exquisite of galleries are those of pictures which were planned but never painted, just as the most luminous of libraries are those of books which were plotted but never penned, so the most delectable of dinners are those which are only dreamt of, and which, disappearing with the thought of them, are never dined. And what a help to humility to be persuaded of such phantom pleasures, to lumber pride, privilege, and precedence into the sphere of fancy, and to console our fretful hopes and peevish ambition by a largesse of realms unruled, libraries unwritten, galleries unseen, and table d'hotes undevoured! And what a joy to know that everything is sifted of its evil and purged of its abatements, that we may be kings without care, artists without toil, scientists without research, and epicures without offence! Allow me the dream of my etcetera, and with an etcetera my table is laid, with an etcetera my dish is abundant, with an etcetera my cup runneth over! And, highest delight of all, with that etcetera I am once more on the banks of the Thames to which not only in the body but also in the spirit, and even in the sequence of paragraphs, I shall be glad to return.

At Sandford I contented myself with tea, as the King's Arms had no alternative that answered to an etcetera or that might have turned expectation into the pleasure of a surprise. What I had was tea, ordered as plain and served so, with such additions as inspired the prose of thanks without however aspiring to the poetry of thanksgiving. Naturally I am not carping, or implying that after a tea at the King's Arms one curtails a grace to God, stints a tip to the maid, and confirms the hearty good-byes with god-speeds perhaps more hearty still. No, I was full-blown, with illusions, and I shall be forgiven when I plead that the last elegance of life never touches the delicacy of a dream, and least of all a dream of the intimacies of the table. Nor must I be understood as despising daily bread which I know is the theme of fervent prayer, though butter is a more worldly wish, whilst jam I suppose is one of the lusts of the flesh. As for cakes I leave them with ale to the fulminations of the puritans and of the prophets, abjuring them as a vanity of the palate and as a vexation of the bowels, and incessantly praying that experience may never again enforce repentance. But let me not repine at the sacred and profane bounty of the tea-table, for tea after all is one of the diviner endearments of our earthly days, to be received as a charity of providence, or rather to be remembered as one of the anonymous gifts of God, Who to the bread of affliction is ever ready to add the butter of absolution and the jam of indulgence, Who mingles milk in our cup of bitterness, tempers it with sweetness, and tones it with the tribute and with the travail of the fields. But he who denies there is indemnity in the drop, let him trudge the towing path for hours, and when tired, let him approve the potion and prove his piety under the restful roof and within the welcome walls of the King's Arms.

But there are also procrastinations in the cup, counsels of idleness, and such toying indulgencies of the tea-spoon as leave the evening no reflection but the mystery of a vanished afternoon. I never have submitted to being a driven finger on the clock of time and moreover I find, what others observe in me and reveal in themselves, that an appetite is very companionable. Merely to content nature is naturally very stoical wisdom, but satiety is a solace of the mind. The spirit is most sprightly when the body is appeased, just as he who follows the deeper studies advances best when the house has retired and when the interruptions and tumults of the day have been stilled into slumber. This was my thought when I renewed the toils of the towing path to Abingdon, and this was the thought which I entered into my diary, where, if the truth be told, my doings are much less honoured than my dreams.

Of Nuneham, from which I anticipated much, I remember little for the light was failing and the trees on the further bank were shrouded in the mist. The afternoon was over, and the view was so faded that everything, the river, the path, and the fields, seemed to be moving on of themselves into the evening. I turned off on to the road and came into Abingdon as night fell. The darkness had lifted a little, and by the light of the moon which was drifting through the ribboned clouds I could just discern the spire of St. Helen's Church. The streets were quiet, and as I no longer felt tired I crossed the bridge and looked back into the town from the further fields. There was nothing to be seen, however, except the spire which was still dimly edged against the moonlit bravery of the clouds, the glowing warmth of the windows glinting in the river, and the sombre uncertainty of the trees and houses and bridges that mingled with the mist or blended with the soft and civil shadows of the night sky. But as I passed back over the Thames I confessed that I had seen a pleasing Abingdon, one perhaps favoured by partial lights and indulged by condescending darkness, yet one that left me in the delight of older thoughts, in the pleasure of new impressions, and in the promise of further remembrances. And though the next day was to make harder discoveries I am glad to have looked through a glass darkly, and to have been honoured less with realities than with the half-revelations of the moon, with the discretions of twilight and with the courtesies of obscurity.

I must also admit another reminiscence of Abingdon from which I am neither able nor even willing to disabuse my mind. It is a painting by Turner, composed a century ago before the landscape had been trodden and trafficked out of its antique tranquillity, when the Thames still had the temper and tone of an untravelled river, and when Abingdon was no more than a habitation for the name. There was little historic rigour in Turner's brush, and he certainly has allowed himself such idyllic leniences of his art as leave Abingdon better recognised in the title than in the theme. The town has been softly suffused away in the misty sunlight, the further bank obscured in the fulness of the foliage and the enveloping haze, whilst a bridge and the church spire, both of which are tinted and diminished off into the distance, are the only persuasions of a built and populated beyond. The foreground however is a very pleasing supposition of the brush, or rather one of life's forgotten brevities such as every day affords and as the meditation of the artist redeems. There is a shimmer of light on the water, and on either side of it, enlivening the darker cast of the canvas, are groups of cattle idling with their drovers in the refreshing shallows, all of them standing in passive rumination of the present, and all of them standing in equally impassive resignation to the past and to futurity. But there is no air of a painted fable in the picture, for behind are some plain barges which are passing upstream and a group of labourers loading another barge at the bank. It is a contrast that commends itself, one that, whilst relieving the scene of the over-refinements of peace and of felicity, adds distinction to the humdrum and admits familiarity to the ideal, a contrast that helps one as much to a faith in poetry as to a respect for prose. Blessed are they, it is said, who believe without seeing, and after walking through Abingdon by the light of day, I was happy to leave it with my faith tested and my respect confirmed.

Poetry has its appeals and prose its provocations, but at Abingdon I was not wholly provoked. Of Wallingford however I entered nothing in my diary but that the place was old-fashioned, its beauty a local prejudice, its interest a secret of the archive, and that the fresh bowers of the river had left me with little appreciation for the faded bays of the town. Though prosperous and though even complacent in prosperity, Wallingford is a poverty spot, giving only what English hotels can afford and taking what a traveller can't. Naturally those who preserve a pedigree preserve their plate, and, by way of hospitality, spare their guests the labour of polishing it. And Wallingford rejoices in its generation. Accordingly the luckless wanderer who orders a dinner or books a bed finds that former boasts are neither proofs of present power nor promises of future performance, and that when he pays, it is not for bounty received but for privilege enjoyed. Let me not, however, be considered as complaining, but rather as indulging once more some after-dinner desperations at finding myself in Wallingford being made the poor blunt of sharp practice, and being left with my purse relieved and my appetite unimpaired.

Wallingford is quiet, but there is a still deeper quiet in the park or Bull Croft as it is called. I went in and must have been sitting there alone for about half an hour before an old man came along, a poor and bent figure, and to all appearances as solitary as the reft recollections of past years. He stopped for a while near where I sat, struggling a look at me in his agitation and waiting till he found breath for a few words. I thought I had perhaps taken his seat and to save him the embarrassment of asking I begged him to sit down. But no, he was just glad to see a young man in the park, and when I told him that it was the most pleasingly peaceful spot on the Thames, he was so happy as to take a seat beside me. Few came into Bull Croft, and he had deemed himself alone in his liking of the quiet walks and the stretch of greenery. It was hard to be an old man, to be left behind both in body and in spirit, and to have no one who would feel with him in the desertion of his days. But now he was glad to know that there were still young men who could find their joy where he found his, who could after all think as he thought, and who could seek society as he did in solitudes and in the unseen. He was not left entirely to the silence of himself, and though the voice of the world might be loudest in public places and on the highway, apparently the wisest words were to be heard in the home of common sights and of common things.

Once more I returned to the towing path and to the solitary trail of my own thoughts. For miles the scenery is flat but far beyond I could see the first spurs of the Chiltern Hills, a line of prettily timbered uplands which closing on the Thames seclude it in long and lonely stretches known only to the rambler and the rower. Breaks there are, all as picturesque as the tracts they divide, such as the villages of Goring and Streatley, and later of Pangbourne and Mapledurham. Though modern they are not modernised, and moreover the novel reds and whites of the villas break in gaily and gratefully on the more spacious green of the fields. They have also something of antiquity, ancient churches and moss-grown mills, quaint cottages and other fragments of forgetfulness lying amid riverside reserves of old trees and grassy walks. Viewed from the bridges or from over the fields they wear an air of having been a domain of dreams in their day, and indeed they are reposeful even now, and still betray touches, in spite of the trampling of tourists and the heaping up of hotels, of their one-time untouched and truly untouchable charm. Their privacy is of the past and as unapproachable, and when we enter them as at Goring Church we find ourselves within those tranquillities of place and of the spirit which are the silent answer of long ages to the loudness of life and to the challenges of humanity. He who turns from the garish glare of the city, will observe such modest emblems in the gloom of the nave, such parables in the loopholed windows that are elevated high up beyond the eye, such allegories in the quaint cabinet choir as enlarge hope and lower ambition, such as give the courage and take away the contumely of the grave. They have, admittedly, all the littleness of ourselves, but in their sanctity is some symbol that we do not come and go unregarded. For the cosmos is not wholly without compassion, and allows a place to the pathos of forgotten brasses, to the hopes of unlettered epitaphs, and to the despair of prayers. Sometimes we may laugh at them in our hour of insolence and of certainty, but the wisdom of men finally grows old, and the judgment against us is to come back again to childhood and to babble of green fields. We have indeed our period of pride, and then as the tree falls so shall it lie.

But the young heart cannot grieve in Goring, and I left it reflecting that the sun was yet high, and that the heather was still green on the hills. I caught some of the gaiety of the thought, felt the high spirits of it in the scenery around me, and confessed to myself that there is no happier path than the one to Pangbourne. In the light of the failing afternoon the Thames assumed a persuasive beauty, and though I had far to go I lingered along its idling lengths of rural elegance and dallied dreamily with the day. There are landscapes that know no time, landscapes that seem in their almost religious repose to span the centuries and to hold under a seal of solitude some tenure of eternity. The past was never so permanent, the present so absolute, the future so assured as in such scenes as these, when the mind is tempted to drift on into days to come, and when the lost and leisured hours of childhood disclose themselves and live again. A frail fence, a solitary tree, the far-off voice of a bird, or a scattered and castaway wisp of cloud have all something of the everlasting, something that has been, something that is, something that will be, but when assembled as here in the universal and stately setting of earth and sky they claim a grander kindred, and in the communication of their character whisper to the wanderer a pensive promise of their own immortality. The glimpse has gone which gave them, the light which lent them their lustre has been utterly dispersed, and though they return only as stray ripples of remembrance over the mind they recall the hour which revealed them and salve again the long-lost society of ourselves.

CHAPTER FIFTEEN

To Marlow with further romantic reflections

It was my fortune, at Reading to meet a commercial who never talked of his trade. I arrived in the evening, and passing a hotel, observed through the curtained window a gentleman in full possession of the sitting-room fire. I might have gone further on, and seen what other hotels the town had to afford, but then here was a fire and moreover a corner seat was vacant. I halted for it was already dark, the pavement was wet with rain, and the wind was rising. One more glance and I had entered, and a few minutes later was sitting opposite my fellow-travelled who was in slippers and still in full contemplation of the blaze in the grate. He was an admirable man, educated, and though silent on himself, of sympathetic views and of humourable understanding. Had he been of stricter temper he might have entered a monastery, but as it was he had fenced his own walks of life, made his breviary of the older poets, and had limited the lusts of the flesh to a newspaper, a faithful dog, and a cheerful fire. Apart from the toy extravagances of tea and crossword puzzles, and his taste in the one was as refined as his practice in the other, I suspected him of only one vice, his profession, which was to persuade others to buy what he in no circumstances would ever be persuaded to buy himself. It was his vice, and I should imagine his cross in life, for though he confessed to having no garden he persisted in speaking of fields and flowers, and seemed in the fall of his evenings to retire to the delight of such thoughts, just as in the remnant of their days Diocletian took to the growing of cabbages and Bathes to the consolations of philosophy. A country cottage was all he required, and as he playes with the poker he followed out his visions in the smoke, or for my better understanding of the contemplated acres outlined them in the ashes on the hearth. Indeed even after the maid had entered and in a finely feminine way had dusted all his designs back into the grate and left the hearth bare he returned to the theme. A house, a garden, and above all flowers. In another I should have felt an affectation, for to revere nature is supposed to reveal nobility, and all men seek to flatter themselves by flattering flowers, but my friend was in earnest. Some believe that without us the daisies blow and the lilies grow in vain, but he believed that without them he had been living in vain himself.

Next morning I had thoughts of seeing Reading which, whilst below the expectations of the past has sufficient for present fame in biscuit factories and nursery gardens, a new university and a football team. I intended the round of them all but chancing to go into the main road whom should I meet but my friend of the previous evening sauntering about as though time itself were on the dole and commercialism were cashiered for ever. After a word of greeting I recalled him to a sense of the responsibilities which he had forgotten, and to thoughts of Reading which apparently he did not care to remember. He had been looking into a florist's window and had been sadly reflecting that it was one thing to let his heart run on flowers and another to intern it in a nursery garden. Whilst he was reserving his little pathos for the fireside, humouring it between lights and fondling it in the ease of his slippers and of his armchair, here in Reading they were exposing it to very public and to very prairie breezes, and he had only to go a few hundred yards to find his romance being wheelbarrowed about, or to see it regimented in rows and marshalled for the market. He felt really aggrieved at being ordered to Reading, for as he pointed out it had always been an ignominy to send men to the plantations, and he asked me to believe that he still prayed for the souls of those who had been transported in the past to Botany Bay. I thought of my own ambition to see the nursery gardens during the afternoon, and was driven to all kinds of disguises, petty perfidies, and whatnot to preserve my faith and at the same time to afford him sympathy. But my deceit was my undoing, I had answered his appeals for the most part with a few syllables of acquiescence, followed naturally by deep silences and suppressions of spirit, but my friend was too honest to have an ear for reservations. He was glad, he said, to have met me. I was delicate enough to admit an equal gladness on my part. He was also glad to have met one who had sympathy for his point of view. I think had he even said compassion I should have agreed. And where was I going? Whereupon reflecting that however indifferently ordered our ways were both in life and in Reading they had to be differently directed then, I replied that I was bound for Sonning. And strange to say so was he. Thus it was that all that I saw of the nursery gardens was a glimpse from the top of a bus, and that the biscuit factory, the university, and the football team were forgotten in the contemplative pathos of old bachelor philosophy.

We came to Sonning which is a pleasing spot, and its quaintly architectured grace, rivered variety, and excelling elegance of landscape soon made up for everything that I had missed at Reading. The past and the present are here very happily blended, the grave consorts with the gay, and moreover, what is peculiar to the Thames and most observable at Sonning, a frail and submissive prettiness is mingled with imperial beauties of scene, a prettiness which, demanding no dues of admiration, surrenders its charm to such as seek it. Perhaps it loses in the toils of the summer season, when beset by boats, thronged by tourists, and distracted by traffic, but I saw it in the unpeopled repose of April, when the waters were waste, the trees bare of birds and of leaves, and when the only life was the life of the coming spring.

Beyond Sonning the hills sank away and I was once more in an open plain of deep meadows and of lonely farms. In fact in my long morning's walk from Sonning to Wargrave, the only ones I met and with whom I exchanged a word were some workmen in a barge. They were fishing but not for fish. They were fishing for stones and the morning's catch I could see heaped up on the stern. It was of gravel, and as the men informed me was used as a top-dressing on the great dustless roads of the south. It was a simple but I suppose a very heavy task. They worked in twos, one turning the winch and the other hauling in the stones, and so they laboured day after day all their lives. Two of them were very contented, but the other two were philosophers who looked very askance at their kind, and murmured against the dispensations of providence. The man at the winch affirmed that money was paid in inverse ratio to the amount of labour performed and drew many disrespectful comparisons between his industry in the boat and my idleness on the bank. I did my best to console him, and finally he admitted that as I had received more education than he had, the arrangement was, if not just, at least justified. I therefore resolved to face him with a dilemma. Did he consider education an advantage? He did. Was my life with education more pleasant than his without it? Yes it was! Well, if I had something which he had not, if I had delights which he was denied, it was he who ought to be recompensed, he who ought to receive more pay and more leisure to make up for what he had missed. He was remarkably struck by this argument, and I observed that it made for even deeper discontent with the worldly order, for long after I had left them I could see them engaged in a despairing debate. They had their reflections and I had mine. Standards of judgment are with most of us things of faith and not of practice, and we are all happy to rest our reasons and to leave the issue to habits of mind.

At Shiplake I had forgotten philosophy and was soon persuaded by the engaging graces of the landscape into more natural emotions. The contemplative plain was behind, and I found myself on a parkland path that ran a-long the shadowed edges of the woodland, past little islands that seemed to drift in the wind, and by waters that went wandering round them, and never finding themselves again. Here the Thames has time for the idler and for itself, leisure even for those stray and wayside delicacies of scenery which stay the step and inform the memory of the wanderer, leisure for solitary rushes, for vagrant ripples by the brink of the river, or for the secluded loveliness of April-blown violets amid the grasses. Above all I had the solace of being alone, attentive only to my own steps and to my own thoughts, and free to allow myself such frailties both of feeling and of fancy as accord with solitude and with the tenderness of our estate in the world. For who in such privacies of the field and of the riverside has not trifled with these reflections, and in forgetfulness of the little destiny of his little days has not followed the fate of floating leaves, traced out the ruffled reflections of overhanging branches in the waters, or regretted the tiny stones which he has. carelessly tossed away into the waves? And who has not felt in these instant. delights of the eye the travail of long hours, or has not seen in the glimpse of an early pink in the dark bracken, or in the slight quiver of a grass in the wind some breviary of his own briefer passage, and has not deemed his life to be as the simple skimming of a sea-gull over the spray? These are the memories which stand out and which stand alone, the memories which loom up larger and larger in the levelling length of the years, and which, appearing neither more distant nor more old, amble amiably along in the imagination like a companionable yesterday. They are the memories that indeed outlive their oblivion, and when the hour arrives that shall assemble us with them, who will not promise himself a returning if only in emblems, dreams, and retrospections, and flatter himself though lost, to be lost amid the elements of everlastingness and the transiences of eternity?

But I am loitering by the way. Shiplake has with its own charm prospects of further prettiness, and as I walked along the towing path I could see far away beyond me the afforested hills of Wargrave and Henley, pleasing uplands which looked very distant in the secretive greys of late spring and under the quietness of the sky. I arrived at the ferry, however, earlier than I had expected and crossed over to Wargrave, which is a true Thames village where an alternation of what is and what was is pleasantly pre-served. We are warned on very divine authority against the putting of new wine into old bottles, and are asked to believe that new patches on old clothes are as rentable as all reparations have proved to be. But Wargrave is seemingly neutral ground, a city of refuge where such indiscretions as I have described escape correction, and where modern villas and old country cots are very amiably neighboured, and where the trees and ivy of the Wargrave that was are quite in rural keeping with the Wargrave that is and will be. There is a church, as ancient as any, and yet cemented by living hands: there are inns as new in appearance as they are old in reputation; and then—I should cross my conscience if I did not speak of it—there is, above all these sanctuaries either for the body or for the spirit, a retreat for both however afflicted, the George and Dragon.

Yes, I say the George and Dragon, and if I favour it with private afterthoughts and honour it with public remembrances, it is not without reason. I had just finished a photograph when a young man who had been observing me approached from behind. He was an affable fellow, whose acquaintance I was pleased to make, and which I hope ever after to maintain. Was I interested in the George and Dragon? Yes I was! Perhaps I was a press photographer? No, but a lecturer, and the George and Dragon was a good subject for a slide. Aha! and he was the proprietor and at once offered me his hand and the hospitality of the Inn. I was to come inside. As a rule I am a very perverse and rebellious spirit, but I am not wholly without my submissions, and can surrender at discretion where the discretion is understood to be mine. So I entered and having assured my host that I had not dined was assured in turn that I should dine with him. I had no objections. First of all we went into the dining room and saw the historic sign which had been painted by eminent artists half a century ago to defray a bill, and which, though weathered and dark, still revealed its old humour. My host was engaged in telling me the story when the dinner came. Did I like soup? The question might have been spared, but a further enquiry as to whether I took fish proved so superfluous that I ordered a second helping before setting about the first His last query however 'Perhaps I liked roast beef?' was such a challenge to my judgment, such a provocation to my appetite, such a defiance to both my taste and understanding combined, that I answered that perhaps six was half a dozen, perhaps twelve o'clock was noon, perhaps he was the proprietor of the George and Dragon, and perhaps, if he brought that beef along, I might venture to remove his doubts - and the beef into the bargain. Perhaps! Yes! Perhaps he liked roast beef as well, and perhaps, if he did, he would regret such a guest as myself, and perhaps he might wish, as he mightily might, that he had served up a 'perhaps' as an entre"e, and limited himself to the gesture of a second course and me to the supposition of it. But no, there was no dilemma about that dinner, and none at all about the destination of it, no hesitations, bewilderments, vacillations, and embarrassments about the chips and the Yorkshire Pudding, no 'I wonder whether' with the sauce, 'I'm afraid I can't' with the sweet, and 'I had rather not' with the coffee. I am always agreeable when my host is even more so, and he an innkeeper, who has the ambition to be not only courteous but kind. Never have I met a man who had such a sense for what is really lustrous in life, not one who had such an eye for those who were truly deserving and such a heart to give what they deserved as the proprietor of the George and Dragon in Wargrave. 'You'll mention the Inn in those lectures of yours!' he said, as I rose to go. 'Mention it! a manifold mention of it, both of the Inn and of yourself in my prayers, ' I replied. My word, not a drum was heard, not a funeral note, as we parted, I heaping benedictions on his head and he piling blessings on mine, he answering the gratitude of a guest with the grace of a host, and I lavishing compliments, which, though truths to me, could only be truisms to himself. And finally after many further benisons, spasms, palpitations, and purple protestations of never to be forgotten regard I went on my way.

Half an hour later I was leaning on the bridge at Henley and looking over at the Red Lion where Shenstone confessed to have received his warmest welcome. It was large and more modern than I had expected, but I was glad to observe that it lay in the thanksgiving shadows of the old church which is sufficient grace for all hospitality. I might have entered the old inn and tempted its celebrity, but it happened that my own warmest welcome at the George and Dragon was just engaging both my inner and my innermost ruminations, and I shrank from taxing conscience and capacity alike when I reflected that a tax on my pocket was equally included. Verily enough for any day is the virtue thereof.

Accordingly I left the bridge and returned to the towing path, for though Henley rejoices in the Red Lion, and though it can lay claim to other hostelries as historical as they are interesting, graced with quaint courtyards and alive with recollections of coaching days, its lustre is wholly of the river. At Oxford we think first of the city, and then afterwards of the Thames, viewing it as a subordinate beauty and an attendant delight, or as just one pleasing prospect in a prospect of pleasures even more superb. At London the Thames loses the loveliness of all but the name, and flows in overshadowed humility amid associations more illustrious, between banks more famous, and under bridges more renowned. But at Henley it is the Thames and the Thames alone that bestrides the scene, a broad and brilliant river unsullied by civilisation and untouched by trade. I felt as I went along the towing path with only the wind and the flowing river as my companions that I had never seen a heaven so open, trees so stately, and meadows so ample, that I had never felt so much freedom for the foot and so much space for the soul as at Henley on that pleasant April day.

Those who follow the flare of fashion and the acclamation of crowds may know of another Henley, and even I who have no dealings in the heavy traffic of small talk was aware of a difference. At the name of Henley the mind runs naturally on the royalty of regattas and on the tensity of sporting events, and it is surprising to come in April and see from a distance the old church spire lying in the uncommuning quiet of trees, fields, and waters. It is the surprise that is felt on coming to a far-famed battlefield of former days. The mind is vibrating with the reckless reminiscences of the past, the blood still pulsating with the impetuous passions that were, the ear re-echoes the clash of arms and the cries of the stricken, when suddenly the scene of these tragic struggles opens up on the eye, and the whole vision vapours away into the stillness of the countryside. Long meadows, spreading elms, quiet cattle grazing in the shade, a cot or two, and that is all. Such were my feelings as I walked from Henley to Temple Island which lay in the distance of its own tranquillity like a fabled Hesperides in midstream. The multitudes had dispersed, and it speaks much for the enduring stateliness of the Thames that they had left no unwept, and thanks to the Conservancy no unswept memorials of their stay. The trees are uncut, the paths unspoiled, the fields free from the litter of illiterate joy. Let those rejoice in the Regatta who will, I am happy to have seen Henley under the quiet sky of an April afternoon.

At Hambleden I met the only ferryman who gave me a ticket, and with it the problem of all future fares was solved. Ferrymen receive a fee, but how much was something about which I was too proud to ask and they too politic to inform me. I have always found them very affable, ever ready to discuss the river, the weather, and themselves, but as touching their duty to me and my due to them they were silent, feeling doubtless that from palaver about pence etiquette excused and human understanding dispensed them. Certainly by leaving the amount to my discretion they displayed no end of their own, and many an idyllic dialogue on the river has concluded in a burlesque of explanatory ignorance on my part and in a breviary of laconic acuteness of theirs. To offer half-a-crown was either to lose it entirely or to receive five sixpences back and evidently copper appeared to abase both my respect and their expectation. I could never escape this anti-climax of cash in our acquaintance, for though in our first greeting at the ferry I felt superior, and in our communings on the river was glad to be an equal, yet in the final exchange of my silver speech with their golden silence I, no less than my purse, looked smaller in my own eyes. Milton says somewhere that they also serve who only stand and wait, and my ferrymen, after rowing me over, would in the approved manner just stand and wait, and thereby serve - and very faithfully - themselves.

So one poor penny was the primum mobile of it all! The price was plainly marked on the ticket, and its humility, emphasised by the age and by the obvious honesty of the ferryman, made me reverse the usual reflection of 'How little dare I offer?' into 'How much should I give?' I answered the query in the spirit of Grace Abounding, and whilst increasing his credit, hope I gained some in his opinion. He was an old man but he seemed very hale and very happy in the fulness of his days, and I naturally flattered his youthful looks as is tactful when speaking to those who will soon no longer be with us. He was unmoved however for he knew men who were older, and when I praised the Thames of those parts he spoke of parts that were prettier and was able to prove their superiority. I saw that in spite of his simplicity he was very wise, for he realised that he was merely one lost drop in the storm of things and therefore he neither expected nor asked more than was his due. I suppose he has long forgotten me, but I still retain the ticket I received, a small yellow slip which opened my eyes to the power and to the penury of simple pennies and loosed me from the toils of many trafficking thoughts. If a man will be virtuous he must cross a Rubicon every day, and yet, such is the grace of life, he may always expect some simple ferryman to spare him the expense of blazing his boats. And the greater the service the less the hire. At Medmenham I crossed the Thames again and viewed the Abbey from the further bank. A labourer who had been working there observed my interest, and coming over to me added such comment as the travelled might never guess nor the guide-book supply. Apparently there is nothing in Medmenham, but what is not of the present day. The cloistered arches, which would recall the old Cistercian sanctities of four hundred years ago, and which would seem to be relics of the long-lost abbey wall, have neither age nor art to commend them. They are modern. They preserve no history, they awake only thoughts of it. Even the window above, which is ecclesiastically pointed, religiously glazed, and enclosed by creeper, is not antique but antiquated, and like the ruins has been deliberately devised. But what matter! Though Medmenham Abbey is as the name it bears a very pretty imposition, bogus in its appeal and spurious in its splendour, it is a spot of venial freedoms, one where illusion may indulge its licences and where thoughts may happily go astray.

My friend the labourer was intimate both with the actualities and with the associations of the scene. He had built or repaired one of the arches, and this familiarity had left him with little respect for the spirit of the building and still less for the price he was paid. He even laughed at the tourists who stood and stared at the arches which he an ordinary labourer had cemented together. I argued that though the admiration of others might be folly it was certainly flattery to himself who on the poorest of pay and with the meanest of materials had helped to attract so much attention and esteem. A portion of the praise was surely his own and even if his work was not ancient there were thousands who thought it so. He had only to believe two things, first that he was no less than his fellows and secondly that no travelled was wiser than his guide, and he might, without any pleas for pardon, stand before his own handiwork and admire. But he simply smiled. There was no value in what was cheap, and he refused to believe that there was any interest in what was new, or any art in what was his. And having never been admired he had neither cause nor excuse for admiring himself.

It is more natural and, it will be admitted, more easy to detect vices than to discover virtues, and my labourer friend was only human when for the pleasure of proving others to be fools he was prepared to admit being one himself. He would feel no shame in such a confession, and doubtless he argued that where all mankind stood equally accused his conscience was acquitted and his guilt, if any, condoned. Perhaps it may evince more benevolence to think that others are better, but it certainly affords more satisfaction to believe that we are no worse, and if we have to blacken faces to prove it we do not shrink from blackening our hands. Indeed the unhappiness of our neighbours is no small part of our felicity, for who has not been consoled in sorrow on learning that he was not alone in misfortune? and has not found his afflictions less on ascertaining that someone had more? It is not wholly envy which repines at the superior luck and character of others, and since those in distress are a solace to those who are spared, we should not wonder that some think worse of their fellows in order to think better of themselves.

At Hurley the Thames breaks away into a multitude of streams and the majestic mood which marked it at Henley disappears. The grander character has gone, but the quieter graces which were so pleasing at Pangbourne and so attractive at Sonning are once more renewed. I stopped at the priory path not far from the bridge, a delicately timbered structure that slenderly spans the by-waters here and appears to be lightly poised on the frailty of its own untroubled reflections. I did not cross it, for through the arches I caught an agreeable glimpse of the island, of its partly meadowed and partly woodland greenery, and of occasional cattle pasturing by the edge of the river. There was an air of privacy in the far fields, something as distant as it was delicate, something of the unattainable tomorrow in the finer aloofness of the scene. Hurley Bridge is very artistic, but it is not the art of the canvas: it is rather the artifice of the cameo, a miniature daintily designed and nicely chiselled, which leaves the thought in suspense as to what might lie in the depths of the precious beyond.

As it was growing dark I turned aside from the towing path and by such light as still remained sought a way through the woods and fields of Temple House. The road is always long where there is little to be seen, and where the mind is naturally kept in constant doubt of the way and in suspense of the destination. Night had already set in when I reached the next village, but I was able to enter the close of Bisham Church, and from the parapet to look up the Thames towards the dimly lit windows of the Abbey. There was sufficient moon to illumine the outlines, to soften the poplars into apparent spires, and to add tones of retirement and of austerity to the woods and waters. It was a view far-off and faint, one that was islanded away into the twilight vacancies of the sky and of the river, and seemingly as removed from the trespass of every foot as from the sacrilege of all sound. But the spirit has approaches, and standing in the overshadowed walks of the church and under the gloom of the tower, I could think myself all the nearer to the lights of the abbey, and could, with reflections on its lingering history, bring the old building into the narrowed intimacy of a thought, and within the space of a whisper. For few of us are proof against the affabilities of the evening, or are indifferent to those familiarities of form and of vesture which darkness favours and which fancy no less than obscurity conspires to supply. So that even the close which had looked grimly in the dusk when I entered it appeared to have lost its severity, and the old church, tempered in spirit and informed with a new benevolence, confessed amid the trees, the walks, and the graves, more quietist communications. The paths and the porch were once more busy with pious speech, the windows renewed their worship, the emblems their remembrances, and the belfry recalled its forgotten chimes. The night of the past had lifted, and on leaving the silence of their speaking society I considered myself no prey to betrayals of the spirit, for who has not an ear for these first and final voices of our being, and has not, in some dull and daylight hour, hoped they would revive, and with the dissolution of times and distances speak again?

CHAPTER SIXTEEN

A close subject and an open discussion

That evening at Marlow as I sat at the hotel fire engaged in writing up my notes of the day, a gentleman came in, and seeing me alone asked if his company were agreeable. I was glad for I dislike no one, though owing to my sense of death I cannot bear importance and pride in human faces: nor endure any of the high airs which many assume, and which, contrasted with their final humiliation, make me believe that life is a fleeting lease of folly, not merely for the fools, but for myself, and for humanity. My friend however had no affectations, but was an ordinary traveller with no desire to appear in any other part than that which from his appearance one might naturally suppose and which he as naturally admitted. He was a man of temperate opinions and of plain expression, and after the usual passage from trivial to intimate topics, I found myself engaging more of his confidences than I had ever thought probable between men so casually acquainted and above all so dependent as we were on the precarious privacy of a hotel fire. Early in life he had become engaged to a consumptive girl, one of good accomplishments and of gravity of character, but who had, by such arts as are better understood than condoned, so concealed her sickness that not till after their marriage was he aware of the nature of her malady. Whether she had expected an improvement in her health or had only been unable to deny herself the last delights of a woman's life he did not presume to know, but finally in middle age he was left without either a home or a child, burdened by the expenses of an invalid and by the bitterness of separation. His distresses had severely frayed his affection, and the regret which he was once content to conceal had turned to a resentment which he did not now fear to express. For time is not to be retrieved, and he certainly is to be pitied who, having lost the independence of youth, is abandoned to the solitude of age.

It is easy to blame when the effects of an act are apparent, when calamities can be traced back step by step to a clear cause and to a single agent. But few when passing such judgments are so philosophical as to enquire whether the several consequences were contemplated or the final event foreseen. It is well to remember that the future is not wholly at our disposal, and whilst it will be admitted that nature is more easily affected by the projects of vice than by the purposes of virtue, there is no one whose plans are a prophecy of their own fulfilment. Responsibility is a very flattering word when the issue is to our honour, and we may reasonably boast of much ability when we prove that the universe is in our hands and futurity at our bidding. To assume therefore that any disaster to the extent both of the loss inflicted and of the victims involved is due to individual design, is to attribute more talent to the offenders than they would themselves venture to claim or we be willing to allow. Intentions, in fact, and not consequences, are the only standard of guilt, and to ascertain these has been the problem of man and the polemic of philosophers for many ages.

My friend was not troubled about the moral niceties of his misfortune, but as he had sought my company he now solicited my opinion. I was in a dilemma, and whilst sympathising with his vexation felt no less for the infirmity of his wife, who, when all is said and done, was one of us, and who in answer to his distresses might plead the heavy pressure of death. Moreover the question was too close to life and I confessed a little alarm at having access to the sacrosanctities of his home, and at being made a partner of those privacies which, when kept unspoken, ensure pride and command respect. For it is no cynicism to say that the only human dignities are in the dark, and that if we are able to care for others and to commend ourselves it is by virtue of what we conceal. In the mercy of these inner mysteries we may enter the society of more honourable men, may be favoured by their influence and elevated in their esteem, while they themselves, secure in secret accounts with God and in reckonings beyond common knowledge, may in all the aggrandizement of their earthly glory take their covered skeletons unsuspected to the grave. For if all were known, and the full inventory of . vices and virtues were paraded on our brows, who would be saved from shame or spared from aversion? Or would not, when abandoned by better men, seek solitude rather than consort with those worse than himself? Speech indeed promotes society but it is silence that preserves it, and as in the obscurity of our careers and characters we may, when afflicted, expect more pity than blame, it is silence also which, by thus upholding the bond of soul to soul, helps to justify the grand injustices of God.

 Apparently I was not responsive enough to my friend, who, used to more sympathy, had finally convinced himself of a grievance, and no less finally convicted his wife of guilt. He thought my ideas a little too innocent for the world and its ways, and after referring to my happy inexperience left me to the safe and fireside reflections of infants and of philosophers. I was not disturbed by his reproach of inexperience, and in answer to his remark that we revise our views under suffering had replied I did not doubt it. When we suffer we are judges in our own cause, and since we always pass sentence in our favour need scarcely wonder why it is harder to persuade others than ourselves. Under suffering opinions are altered but impartiality is not improved, and when emotions are privileged morals have neither pride nor place. It is natural that those who have failed in marriage should turn from the drudgery of duty to the delights of divorce and having accommodated their conscience should commandeer that of society. And it is natural also that society when driven to the dilemma either of heightening the law and enforcing virtue or of lowering it and allowing vice, should choose the less perilous and more expedient way. Having assumed that to govern is not a question of ethics but of convenience it winks at inward duties, and on the pleasurable principle of establishing credit by abolishing debts, or of restoring an army to discipline by releasing it from obedience, proceeds to enact dead letters to please us all.

Afterwards as I sat alone before the dying fire, I felt that I had learned little of the art of life. Though my friend had given me his confidence and even opened his ear to persuasion, his sorrow when he went away was not less nor his power of bearing it more, and whilst in the debate he had been defeated I could entertain no hope at all that he would admit it to me or confess it to himself. The hearth was mine, but the friend who had shared it was gone, and moreover it was too late to replenish the fire. I shivered it over my notes a little longer till the landlord came in and exchanged a word with me. He was more an adept in the plain politics of life than myself, and observed, as he looked at the last flicker in the ashes, that the weather had been warmer of late. Out of kindness I agreed, and so pleased was he with my compliance that when I ventured later to say it was chilly of an evening I won both his assent and a call to the maid for more coal. I am certain now that had my friend found any kindness in me, he might have discovered some to his wife, and then, with the knowledge that his confidences were in safe and friendly keeping, have secreted his criticism and opened his mind to other thoughts. I concluded that it matters really little what we think as few think very clearly, and those few live for the most part in hourly violation of their views. It is enough if we agree, for social commerce is not only without price but without expense, easily carried on with the well granulated sugar of compliment and poverty spice of politeness, and though we all welcome grander cargoes, gifts, sacrifices, and heavy offerings of earth, our joy is no greater than that of those who, when a birthday is remembered, rest their souls in words and wishes, breathe in happiness from the air, revel in the post-haste scribble of remembrances, and build castles of ecstasy on a card.

CHAPTER SEVENTEEN

Digressions from the path

On leaving Marlow I had the choice of two paths, one along the river, and the other through Quarry Woods over the hill to Cookham. I took the latter in the expectation of broader prospects, and, amid the alternations of woods, farms, and villages, of more variety of view. The uplands are always pleasing, but most so in the spring when the foliage is in bud and when the bold outlines of the branches still lend loftiness and breadth to the bare trees. In the long slender length of the trunks and boughs the beeches and elms appear more noble, the creeper more graceful in contrast with the leafless greyness of the woods and walks: the stones, walls, and cottages darker and more aged in the subdued light of the early year. The cumber of the summer greenery has gone, and even in the most shadowed depths of the forest the eye has easy access to the sky and clouds, and the ear, awake to the echoes in the wind, freely receives the first voice of the birds, or piously responds to the bells vibrating far away in the valley. There is a gravity as well as a gaiety in the landscapes of spring, when the peeping buds vividly reveal the ravage of the winter storms, and when the frail and fragrant promise of the primroses is unfolded amid the still littered and trampled testimonies of the departed year.

The road to Cookham was unattractive, but I still had expectations of the river. The ferryman at Hambleden whilst allowing my praises of Pangbourne and my hosannas of Henley told me to reserve my preferences till I reached Cliveden Woods. As I came down to the river near Cookham I admitted their dignity for there is an air of religion in such embowered recesses of the Thames, something of worship in the woods and of piety in the waters as they flow along this cathedral aisle of the trees and hills. But the attractions of scene are ill consorted with the travesties of association, and history has apparently been as unkind to Cliveden as to Medmenham itself. The estate was first held by the dissolute Buckingham who by all accounts was so debased a blood that when Dryden in the bitterness of satire attempted a caricature he could only achieve a portrait. While Buckingham's character however is not to be commended, his taste is not to be despised, and if he knew not how to live he knew where. The same might be said of the no less licentious Frederick Prince of Wales, who to the gratifications of sense united those of power, for it was here that 'Britannia, rule the Waves' was first sung. Whether this was understood of the billows of the ocean or of the ripples of the Thames is not now to be determined, and as the estate has since been bought by American millions it would be more consoling not to enquire. Paradoxical it is that while we are triumphant on all other shores we are trespassers on our own, and whilst advancing everywhere with the flag and fleeing everywhere from the notice-board we add to the infamy of persecuting others the folly of prosecuting ourselves.

 Two miles further on I intruded into one of the superb suburbias of London, Maidenhead to be exact, a place of plutocratic prettiness, and one where everything plebeian is a long social remove from the river. Maidenhead is modern and lives by virtue of its modernity, a town forgetful of the past and indifferent to the future, and, if my hasty survey allows me to speak, idly dependent on the delights of the present day. Not that Maidenhead is given to Babylonian persuasions, far from it, but taste outweighs all tradition there and pleasure precedes business. Its patrician air was borne on me as I came along from Cliveden for though the residences were retired from the bank, each owner had an exclusive entrance to the river, a private bridge and a personal barge. I do not doubt that their one grievance is the towing path, which is a great violation of their plutocratic privacy, and which divides them by a still greater violation from the finer plutocracy of the Cliveden estate. I stepped on to one of the stages to take a picture and had to endure the insolence of the owner. He was obviously of very upstart prosperity, one of those who for business reasons are polite in the City and for social reasons impertinent at home. Moreover he had a dog, and as such animals partake of the prejudice of their lord, and frequently of the pants of those who offend him, I did not reply. I am only poor and a pedestrian, and shall, by neither privilege nor profession, be a bargee.

Of Taplow I have no other impression than the affluence of the place and the aloofness of the people, but barely two miles beyond its modernity I chanced on crossing the river into one of the lingering yesterdays of Southern England, the village of Bray. It has no loveliness of landscape to commend it, none of the wooded depths of Cliveden nor the watered daintiness of Sonning, and offers nothing to the eye of the approaching traveller save plain fields, ambling paths, and a vacant river. But Bray has tradition and though by vicarious fame it is known for pendulum opinions, fluctuating faiths, and elastic loyalties, it has been left up to our own day unaffected by fashion, and unruffled by the rush of reformations and of years. The houses are ancient, the church without publicity of approach, and the vicarage is so removed from view that rural heresies and fugitive beliefs might, with little suspicion and less shame, come and go unheeded. That Bray was once a haven of easy ecclesiasticism is to be understood, and as long as the vicarage is preserved might even now afford a privacy and a by-path to phlegmatic ambitions and to quiescences of conscience. The ancient vicar, when indulging his lease of precarious ease, was not without excuse, and no one need wonder why, holding to that which was good, he lived on in the fulness of his beliefs and died finally in the emptiness of his days. The world has allowances: every offence has its forget-fulness; every sin its absolution, and while the commoner may look forward to the repose of a sabbath, the clergy may lie back in the relaxation of a living. And rightly. For why should the shepherd leave the proffered fatness of the fields, when the sheep perversely pasture in the towns? Verily where the harvest is great the labourers will always be few, and more verily still, where the labour is greatest the pay is universally least.

To photograph the church I required permission, but on applying to the vicar was told he was away in Maidenhead. His absence might have made the labour easy to easier consciences than mine, but I am a good citizen, and can live up to dead letters and can honour the ordinances even in the dark. I returned and sat down near the devotional lights of the choir but for some inner reason I fell into profaner reflections. From thinking of the old vicar of Bray, I took to thinking of many modern vicars I had met, men who reposed on velvety faiths and on plushy beliefs, and who possessed, amid other perquisites of the spirit, both a proxy for their crosses and a pocket for their crowns. I became involved in comfortable thoughts, for our vanity is founded more on the vices of others than on the virtues of ourselves, and consoled by the feeling that everyone is bad we condone the fact that we are no better. Every century has its sins, I argued, and every man his iniquities. What does my idle drop matter in the common storm? The afternoon was calm and bright and I wondered if I could take a photograph, and as the thought stole upon my interest I somehow found the camera in my hand. It would take a long exposure was my next reflection and my tripod opened out of itself. It was an easy subject, I observed, and the film was in. 'Of course,' I said, and the picture was taken. It was not done however without fear and trembling, for a child entered, and after some talk I discovered its innocence more than a match for my iniquity. As is natural I shrank from the respect it freely gave me. I left the church convinced that it is an aid to virtue to believe well of our neighbours, for without example there can be no emulation, and without emulation no morality, and when once we begin to examine the consciences of others we are no less ready to explain away our own.

A short distance from the road is the Jesus Hospital, an institution founded by William Goddard, who according to his monument in the church was formerly of the mystery of the fishmongers. On entering I was met by the old lady at the door, perhaps one of the inmates, but certainly one of reflective reading and of approvable humour. I asked her whether the fishmongers were really so mysterious, and with an innuendo that mystery is the handmaid of power she replied, 'Well, they dominate our little world.' She then told me of the life there. Bray is now either too small or too prosperous to provide forty poor people and many come from other parts. From what I saw of some of them they seemed of the politer sort, with proofs of breeding, and I suppose with recollections of elegance. I looked into the chapel and on asking my guide whether it contained anything of interest was informed, 'Well, it is old. ' At my further question, 'Is interest a characteristic of age?' she smiled, and I shall not forget her answer. 'Of ourselves perhaps not, but of chapels it seems to be.' I understood, for she was no less alive than resigned to the irony that while God is no respecter of persons, man is only no respecter of them when they are old.

So Jesus Hospital was not for the sick as I had thought, but a seclusion of cottages for the aged poor. The entrance is impressive, but beyond it is a quiet quadrangle of gardens around which are ranged the low quaint houses of the aged community. According to the bequest each tenant delights in the independence of his own chimney, but lest he feel the solitude of it, there is always the quadrangle where both in aspects of his garden and in prospects of gossip he may escape for a time from the retrospects of perhaps happier days. There is no air of an almshouse about it, though the outer gate is closed at ten, drunkenness is frowned upon, and riotous behaviour with vanity and profanity of language is visited with official displeasure. Naturally when one is old, when the passions have abated and the blood has bubbled down, such rules add nothing to the heat and burden of well-sheltered days. Owing to the poverty of the inmates, drunkenness is impossible, owing to their age fighting is too laborious, and it will be admitted that neither emptiness of pockets nor plentitude of years are the means whereby tipsiness, uproar, and nightly campaigning are supported. I felt as I bade my gracious guide good-bye that there is even bliss in being old, at least in the Haven of Refuge at Bray, where one perforce must throw bones of contentions to the dogs and sell apples of discord for copper considerations, and where, with the realisation that politics and philosophy are simply the spiritual ping-pong of ignorance and academics, one finds no other use for burning questions than in all good-humour to light the pipe of peace.

Before leaving Bray I was drawn once more to the church, and, as no one was there, sat for a while in the afternoon privacy of one of the pews. There is elevation in the Church of Bray, a light abandonment in the aisles and the arches, and such happiness of illumination as mellows away the severity of form and austerity of shadow which it is the aim of religious art both to deepen and to subdue. Yet with all its simplicity of form and transparency of design, there are graver casts, and he who looks down the prayerful avenue of the nave, or lingers in the ascetic ecstasy of the choir, or pores over the surviving syllables on the tombs, the busts, and the brasses will not fail to find the darker sequestrations of the spirit, nor despair of those untroubled retirements which favour the final reflections of life and death and lasting judgments. But let me indulge no elegiac thoughts of Bray Church, which though of little epic repute is a place of lyric loveliness, delightful to the idler, exquisite to the scholar, and affording to them who still hold to the old beliefs happy reflections on the past and still happier confirmations of futurity.

Whilst in Bray I fell in with a motorist who regretted that I should have passed by Burnham Beeches, and should, out of a perverse affection to the towing path, perhaps even neglect a glimpse of Stoke Poges. The old country churchyard where Gray wrote the Elegy and where his tomb was still to be seen ought to interest one of my tastes, and my friend began to recite many stanzas, though whether to prove his knowledge or remove my ignorance it would be vanity to enquire. I had really intended walking on to Windsor, and might with a meek acceptance of all his criticism have gone my own way but that he offered to take me to Burnham in his car. He was in any case returning to Beaconsfield, and as the woods lay in the way and my company seemed agreeable to him I allowed myself to be persuaded. He drove at a perilous speed, and in the animation of his talk looked anywhere but where he was going, so that he doubled every bend on two wheels, and took corners with one toot and such a stampede across that the ride afforded me great pleasure in surviving it. I was glad to alight at the Beeches, and declined after a cursory run round to be taken on to the Churchyard of Stoke Poges, for it is a plain observation that he who hastens as a visitor prolongs his stay as a guest, and I had no desire that my first call should be honoured with a final reception. My friend was not annoyed, and in his character as a motorist appeared in fact more flattered by my fears than offended by my refusals, and after chatting for a leisurely half-hour which might with more safety and more profit have been spent on the highway he careered off to Beaconsfield.

 We have few forests, and such wide stretches of woodland as invite the foot and allure the eye in Germany are here unknown. Burnham Beeches however has titles to esteem, and though it pretends to no extent presumes to some antiquity. Certain of the trees are said to be of great age, and their girth conspires with the guide-book to confirm this assertion. I know nothing of trees, but were I asked in all privacy for my opinion I might with a clear conscience say they were three hundred years old. Seeing however that I lecture abroad and that it is expedient and proper to bang the big drum of my native land, I dare not stint the centuries and allow these trees less than half a millennium. But were I talking to Americans I should be even more expansive, and were I a liar I should open up the floodgates, indulge the tide of time, boast of Domesday Book, and put every beech down at a thousand. At first I was impressed by Burnham Beeches, but unlike a German woodland, it offers refreshment only to the eye. I wandered for hours and saw nothing more hospitable than barbed fences and nothing more edible than pollarded beeches. I could not help but observe that as my hunger waxed their age waned. I decided that I would never be a liar on their behalf, and add sins to my account by adding ciphers to theirs, nor would I, even when faced by the most magnificent of Americans, seek to oppose the sky-scraping height of their buildings by the creation-scraping age of our trees. The more I famished the more I found reasons for believing that every stick in the forest had been recently planted, and when parched and fainting I finally arrived on the highway I concluded that the babes in that wood at least were no other than the beeches themselves.

In spite of the late hour I found my way to Windsor, but next morning I returned to Stoke Poges. It is as easy to imagine what I expected as what I experienced. In my views of men and things I hold to the older fashion, and am apt to forget when reading the literature of long ago that the centuries have their curfew no less than each departing day. Perhaps I am not alone in these loitering thoughts, and maybe many have gone to Stoke Poges with grave and evening anticipations of the old churchyard, with visions of a glimmering landscape fading on the sight, and with reveries of aged thorns, mouldering heaps, and ivy-mantled towers. And yet doubtless there are many more, modern men and materialists, who would number me with such moping owls as complain to the moon of their own midnight imagination that the world has not left them to a world of darkness and to themselves.

The vicar whom I visited was very kind, but certainly not a man of elegiac appearance, of country character, or of churchyard associations. He was young and athletic, and I soon discovered that in Stoke Poges the knell of parting day was less regarded than the toot of his approaching Ford. Nor was the church in better poetical case, stormed as it was by tourists, beset by photographers, and littered by films. It has become a haunt of money changers, a place of business, one where it is easier to purchase a booklet than to peruse a bible, to buy a postcard than to offer a prayer, one where the Testament has been forgotten and the Elegy alone remembered, and where all are less disposed to serve a sacrament of Christ than to sell a souvenir of Gray. No, there is no devotion in Stoke Poges, for there is no congregation, there are no prayers for there are none to pray. The vicar has his living, the verger his tips, and the sexton his sinecure, whilst all a-round the modern and multitudinous homes of Socialist workmen have paganised the scene.

Before I left the verger insisted on my photographing the porch. He was young, obliging, and a gentleman, and I suppose in season of no small credit in those parts. His enthusiasm was great though, as regards the porch, his information was of the faintest. The porch was old, he told me, it was known to be old by the vicar, and no one who had seen it, not even those who were able to judge, had ever denied its title to age. It was made of solid pieces of oak, though where the oak grew, and how long it flourished, or when it was felled, he had no precise knowledge. But it was ancient, perhaps as ancient as the church itself, the foundation of which history ascribed to the twelfth century, and sentiment to a date even earlier. Amiable estimates, which I for reasons less amiable did not trouble to dispute. So in all docility I took the picture and prize it still, not as the verger for business reasons as a way into the church, but simply for pious reasons as a way out of it.

CHAPTER EIGHTEEN

The last phase

My way to Windsor lay past Eton, and I spent half an hour in inspecting the school, the chapel, and the library. Cynical of all celebrity as I am I entered with a certain reserve, for age is no warrant of excellence, and the fame of most schools, like, I suppose, much of their learning, is involved in fables. Not that Eton is more dubious than others for even Oxford itself I had come to regard as a grandiose convention, and had wondered where in the succession of colleges, tangle of quadrangles, and plenitude of spires, there was any compulsion to be wise. Indeed in such a place inducements to dulness are not wanting, and as for indolence mere opportunity is enough without the urge of persuasions. It is felt by most students that antiquity, without any further quality to commend it, is a safe-conduct to public regard, and that as long as they may boast of association with a name, they are dispensed from proving any inspiration of the spirit. Content with the cumber of credos and acceptations of which history, vanity, and higher education are made up they flatter themselves with an atmosphere, presume on the past and assume they are partners in its fame, and cocker with the company of the ghostly exalted and suspect no exclusion. As spiritual hangers-on of the great, and as crumb-scrambling lazars round the tables of distinction, they soon become adepts in dust-bin economics, and are early aware that possession of a first edition is more valued than appreciation of the last, that a name on a wall is more attractive than renown in the world, and that having bought the mantle of a prophet they may then parade the mentality of a publican without reproach and without remorse. For there is no more thrifty traffic than the pious one of rags and relics, and he who invests in it may well afford a slump in salvation.

It is a sad observation, and yet on reflection a reassuring one, that of all human virtues, only the lack of them is hereditary. Powers we have, but how to apply them must be won from experience, and whilst in their application is all wisdom, in their disposal is all virtue. Property may be passed on, and money goes from man to man, and man from dust to dust, but ability is not to be bartered, and the rout of pretenders have in all ages found that talent is easier to assume than to acquire. Portionless themselves they take to trading on the testaments of others, and accordingly when genius is dead its estate is entered upon, parcelled out among the parasites, and either turned into preserves for polite and proprietary conversation, or farmed out to such as pose the favours of the spirit. The property is then fenced in by the multiplied hocus-pocus of a critical apparatus, the meaning immured behind embankments of interpretation, till finally the plodders may, within the ramparts of research, erect little exclusive kingdoms, and there in all sovereignty may palaver in their parliaments, demand dues of all entrants, and enjoy undisputed obeisance by virtue of sceptres they have never wielded and of crowns they have never worn. And whilst I must not be understood as tilting at the task of an editor, it will be admitted that when he sounds the onset he soon has the pack in full halloo around him.

But to return. It would be idle of me to speak of Eton since I can boast of having seen no more than a school without scholars, a library without students, and a chapel without a congregation, nor would I presume to speak of those after such a brief view on a vacational afternoon. I had to include much in a glance, for the attendants were in haste and the Provost due any minute. Apparently he was in deep literary labour, and so reverent was the library assistant in his allusions to this that I was led to believe that another Testament was in adumbration and that a second annunciation of the spirit was expected. With time for neither examination nor reflection I was hustled as through a Woolworth welter of select assortments, shown the treasures of the library, manuscripts, incunabula, and first editions, though why these, surely the worst printed and the least read, should be the most highly prized I have never understood. To say they are rare is the fallacy of conversion, for scarcity is a characteristic and not a condition of value. And were an example needed let us cite the Fire of London, which was not only rare but unique, though no one but fools and makers of mischief would pray for its repetition. Naturally I know the dialectic of both sides but I still wonder why, when reprints are available, the mouldering originals are not consigned to the flames.

Whilst in the library the attendant drew my eye to some charters, and it was a humiliation to see that formerly when signing documents great men were content to put a cross in lieu of writing their names. I suppose writing was not so much above their powers as beneath their dignity, and since war and the chase were the callings of a hero the caitiff practice of letters was left to slaves. Such a fact might well abate our pride, for what was the fashion of the past might easily be the fashion of the future, and we who look back with contempt on those who could not write will in turn be despised for having written so much. Centuries ago it was a proof of power and breeding to be able to drive oneself and to engage a scribe, nowadays the proof lies with him who can ply a pen and hire a chauffeur. And who will be so bold as to deny that, amid the vagaries of taste, fluctuations of fashion, and inconstancies of habit, the sciences and arts might again be cast away to the clerks, and that he alone will evince nobility who can drive his car, mend the wireless, and adjust the electric light?

After strolling round the town and fields I left Eton with the impression that its one talk and only interest is itself. In others this might be insolence, but in Eton it is the prostrate fate of those who must live by being obliging to strangers and obsequious to boys, and who in this underling intercourse with the world find no place for the practice of the needful superiorities save on themselves and their friends. They were all very helpful but there was a pathos in their politeness, and how could it be avoided when to belaud others they must belittle what is theirs, and when to the business of humility they must add the belief that there is no better? From dwelling in the shadow of the great they have come to forget that the sun shines on the evil and on the good alike, and that the rain blusters over the crowned and uncrowned heads of us all.

It was the same at Windsor where I observed that everyone was too aware of it, and that however busy they might be all were very conscious of the castle and of the residence of royalty. This may escape other visitors, but coming as I did from the April solitudes of the Thames and from the abandonment of the towing path, I was made to feel that mankind had other preoccupations than the landscape and the sky. There was an air of peopled expectation at the castle gates, portents in the movements of soldiers and officials, and there was no less suspense at the approach of cabs and motors than gazings and ruminations long after each had departed. The police reveal an eye for the visitor, the shopkeeper his pent-up anticipations, the taxi-driver his Good Samaritan interest and guile. Everywhere from Eton College to the Castle wants are read before they are expressed, doubts removed before they are ever indulged, and the idler who would love to drift in the idleness of his own meditations is finally fingerposted into the spacious privacy of the Great Park.

If solitude be the despair of a commoner it must be the sigh of a king who cannot escape from the curiosity nor excuse himself from the criticism of anyone who chooses to abuse either. His only pleasure as a man is his praise as a monarch, and his only pleasure as a monarch is that the foe might press on the bombardment and prosecute the siege with unflagging vigour. With such a reflection I should have been afraid to enter the Castle had it been open to visitors, and was therefore glad to congratulate my conscience that it was closed. In spite of my diffidence however I saw the very man whom I deemed it a courtesy and an unsuspected service to avoid. I was standing in High Street, when a passer-by drew my attention to a gentleman in a car which had been stopped by a block in the traffic. He was not more than a yard or so away, and I found myself looking at him and him at me. He had, what is so agreeable to see in men of position, frail and familiar features, a face which, despite the aping admiration, parrot hypocrisy, and lionising loyalty of empires, was still informed with the human humilities that publicity hardly ever fails to dispel. Naturally to withstand the reproaches of enemies is not above human virtue, but to bear up against the praises of friends is divine, and he who with a full conscience can endure adulation may defy adversity. That the King has endured so long with so little alienation in his looks is a distinction, for royalty must rack the modesty of any nature such as his which regards power as a responsibility, dignity as a trust, and applause as a spur to deserve it. I had only a glimpse of him however, and when a moment later his martyred mortality moved off into the immensity of the castle, passing out of view as it were like a fallen and flitting leaf into the waste of the forest, I wondered what delight there could be in a life where the paths are appointed and the privacies publicly policed, and where even the solitudes are sentinels on themselves.

A king and a castle, whilst affording a contrast, provide a comment on one of the fondest fallacies of mankind. It is as old as error itself, and as habitual, and seemingly the gates of Hell and of education cannot prevail against it. I shall choose an easy illustration from Beowulf where the fault is frequent, and where the puerilities of thought are emphasised by the pretensions of speech. Beowulf, the old Gothic hero, after quelling the monsters that preyed on the Danes, took leave of the king and then went to the coast to sail for home. On his arrival at the shore, the coast-guard who had kept watch over the ship in the absence of Beowulf went to meet him. They greeted each other, and according to epic custom Beowulf offered the coast-guard a reward. He gave him a sword, a precious sword bound with gold, and he gave it him for a reason. And the reason? He gave him this present, in order that when drinking with his companions the coast-guard might be the more esteemed, that he might be the more appreciated because of the ancient weapon, and take precedence by property. They would think him a better man, because he had a better sword, they would think he had a better heart because he had a better coat. It is a confusion of standards. We cannot measure the moral worth of a man and the material worth of his walking stick together by the same scale. We cannot measure a pound of cheese and a pint of milk on the same balance at the same time. I am no taller than my neighbour because I have money in my pocket. I am no richer than he is because I see head and shoulders above him. Put in this way it may appear a very barbarian error, a bib and napkin blunder which we of a later age have set aside, and yet it would be hard to indulge a judgment not tainted by this mistake. It is the cement of every stone in Windsor Castle, it is the tenure of every acre in Windsor Park, and by virtue of it we commend our souls to God and ourselves to the guns and to the guards of government. Indeed where the right of rule is not of merit as in very early times, but, as in all modern nations, of birth, prescription and lottery, we are forced to seek for the respective sanctions of all three in titles, ostentation, and talk, and to rely for homage not on truth and virtue but on secrecy and show. For by exhibitions we are able to deceive the mob of minds, and by mystery we induce them to deceive themselves, and society slumbers at peace in the assurance that principles are of less avail than the belief that they are maintained. Naturally such assurance is easy with the help of dress and decorations, but were these abolished and had we to prove ourselves in all our nakedness to the world who would be masters among us?

Windsor Park is one of those excepted landscapes where the eye may rest but where the foot must wander, and where trespass is the price of repose. One might, I admit, indulge the grass even on the Long Walk, and the law will saunter genially by without a protesting word. It is a liberty however, one which wants authority, and which, resolving into a persistent lying down in the body and a perpetual getting up in thought, ends up as all precarious pleasures in spiting itself. It could be answered that he who accepts grace should not lack gratitude, nor gaze askance at that which though freely offered might with equal propriety be refused. Where the entrance is free the exit is no less without price, and what choice continues choice may conclude. Still I hope I am offending neither taste nor truth when I say that the frontiers of the Park are more widely set than the pales of fatigue, and that when the foot is weary the mind halts between claiming the gifts of God and acclaiming the courtesies of a king. Admiration of the estate yields to envy of the deer, which freely take covert in the woods, hollows, and long grasses, and the noblest seat in the island is remembered only as not having afforded one to the passer-by.

Leaving the Park I turned aside to Old Windsor which can boast nothing more than the persuasions of a name, and I at last came to the Thames again near the celebrated inn, The Bells of Ouzeley. I forgot its public air, its thoroughfare approach, and the advertisement shadow of the trees, and hoped that the old hotel was famous for what it offered and not for what it appeared. Of the nature of its fame I know nothing nor when seated inside sipping my refreshment was I any better informed.

But it is famous. It is mentioned in all the guide-books, it is mentioned by all the guides, and travellers have talked tradition round the spot and round themselves. It is famous and it is old, but just as I was able to learn nothing about its fame, so I was left unenlightened about its age. It was old, said the proprietor, how old he did not know, nor would he convulse my belief by guessing, but of its fame he had no doubts, and he was glad to meet one who shared both his company and his convictions. Queen Victoria, he added, always drove past the Bells of Ouzeley, which seemed to me a doubtful compliment, but perhaps she would have alighted and rejoiced in the genialities of the old inn had Windsor been farther away and contemporary opinion on pubs less precise. If the Bells of Ouzeley however has nothing else it has a name, a name with a lilt in it, a name with rhythm and romance in it, a name that deserves to be famous and old were the building never so new and and the proprietor never so young. Even at this distance of time I have my leisured recollections of Wind-sor and of Windsor Great Park, of its ample elms and baronial range of woods and fields, but whenever I desire to indulge them I think first, not of Windsor nor of the Castle, but of the quaint and tuneful title of the celebrated inn, The Bells of Ouzeley.

Near the Bells of Ouzeley, just beyond the pale of its convivial fame, is a spot of more ancient though perhaps less authentic renown, the official font where we were baptised into our official freedom - Runnymede. In several lands such places vary according to political and religious persuasions, and many believe that liberty began where others with equal sincerity lament its conclusion. In Germany some are pledged to Würtemberg, and speak of the boulders of Papal oppression which were rolled from the European breast by Luther, and some have memorialised their emotions round the battlefield of Leipzig and commence their calendar of liberty with the flight of the French army. But our anthems are undivided, and from the cradle to the grave we frown on all duetted enthusiasms, and stifle every rivalling antiphon to our one solo celebration of Magna Carta, a testament which, while allowing us to applaud our ancestors and to approve ourselves, helps history to a little halo, fact to a little filigree, and patriotism to bun-loaf and apologies. And our faith in it advances with the blackening of the type in the books.

Philosophy has its fashion and facts have their phases, but principles keep their feature for all time. Save in the primitive days when governance by God was prescribed and acknowledged, men have had no constitutional differences but the two decided by the Charter and debated ever since. The polity that humanity has always sought and tyranny overthrown is one where there are no taxes without just cause or general consent, and where there is no punishment without popular knowledge or a public trial. Despotism has only two spheres, our pockets and its own prisons, and a community may well be content when the cash and the keys are in good and legal keeping. In early and more arbitrary ages even the boldest when taxed would dare to ask a despot no more than 'How much?', but when tyranny had lost its terrors it was not rebellion to ask 'What for?', and finally with both parties equal in law and balanced in power finance occasioned no quarrel but as to who should spend it. It is an easy evolution, one which common sense might guess and daily life abundantly illustrate, and historians might with advantage spare themselves the labour of research and schoolboys the slavery of remembering that about which better observation of each other would leave them better informed. Magna Carta is said to have been signed on the island. Tradition admits it and all Englishmen are pleased to concur save the exact historians who ignoring the tablet which says so and the table on which John yielded assent affirm that the treaty was signed on the bank. The story, if memory serves, is that the river divided the contending armies, and that the island afforded neutral ground just as Napoleon and Alexander met on a raft in the Niemen before arranging the Peace of Tilsit. However that may be, it is good when well-grounded in ignorance to have a nod for all knowledge, to be all things to all men, neutral to none, and to serve both science and superstition with such reverence as to make of every mistake a mystery and of every truth a dispensation for doubt. Thus having taken a picture of the island I honoured the exacter historian by taking one of the meadow also, feeling in my divided devotion to romance and research that perhaps plain truth was in keeping with neither. And if this be reckoned as cynicism let me multiply my moreovers by saying that I have no joy in ancestral triumphs since a celebration implies that had abuses continued we should not now have been able or brave enough to abolish them ourselves.

Being in doubt as to the identity of the island I spoke to a motorist who had parked his car on the green. He was an intelligent man, interested to learn that there was an island in the river, and admitted that amid the residues of schoolboy erudition he had odd and shredded recollections of King John and a Charter. Apparently there was something that the king had offered or the people enforced, but save that it happened long ago my friend knew nothing more than that the event was a big one in the books and a cause for rejoicing. He defended his indifference by quoting his ignorance of the charters of to-day, and was happy to be left unenlightened so long as he could buy and sell at a market price, drive unmolested on the roads, and be master of his own door. He concluded by saying that good government was such as left him alone and as induced others by fear, interest, or moral instruction to do likewise.

This is true when the social services are a charge on the charity of citizens and not on the offices of state, or when public needs are met as they arise by private zeal. Nowadays with the socialising of life, state and society are coincident and anyone may justly be accused of egotism who thinks that protection is all he should expect or the nation afford. My friend had something of logic in his talk and I was about to answer him when the rain which had long been threatening broke down upon us. We retired to the car and as there was nothing to detain either of us in Runnymede we drove on in the downpour to Staines. I should have alighted but for my friend's enquiry as to where I was for, and on his learning that I was making for London on foot he assured me we should be there in an hour or so. There was no gainsaying him for he was a practical man, one who never wandered from the highway, and who, missing none of the milestones of life, reckoned only with results and halted only in destinations. He had doubtless heard of the towing path, but to converse with him about it and to speak of trudging along it in the rain would have lost me his regard, and I had no desire to intrude on his astonishment. Moreover in the course of our talk he revealed himself as a man who had well calculated his corn, and he boasted with no small pride of having an eye for the good ground, of reaping everywhere a hundredfold, and of wasting nothing on the wayside of his days. Ever since the war he had been gazing over the well-propertied prospects of life, and obsessed by his obviously big and barndoor ambitions he let fly his blunderbuss at even the least feather of infringement of his hedges, fields, and trees.

Prosperity loves to speak of itself and as we throbbed along the rain-pelted roads I felt what poverty the best of fortune would be were it not displayed, and how downcast we should appear in triumph were there none to share the pageant and none to begrudge the pleasure of our success. My friend was not above the frailty of self-applause, and having a superior car to others he afforded me proofs of its speed, and enjoying elegant acquaintance in the city he mentioned their quality, and confident of his credit with financiers of standing he expanded on future schemes, planning profits for himself in multiple figures and lumping losses of no less moment on all who ventured to rival him. He carried on to the top of his business bent, and I as much to humour his vanity as to safeguard my own allowed the landscape to look very superfluous in the storm, so that by the time we reached the city I had let all my illusions slip out into the discomfiting and dripping darkness. I had seen the greenery go from the woods, and from the fields, and from the rural reserves of the river, and after advancing deeply into the depravities of the town, amid the costermongered lustre of the lamps and the night-lights, and through the distracting turmoil of trafficking voices, I knew that my friend had come at last into his longed-for home and that my own journey was over.

CHAPTER NINETEEN

Conclusion

It is in the nature of diaries to be more forgetful than ourselves, and there are few that do not leave us indulging long and longing guesses in the gaps or that fail to be most effusive where we are most informed. We glance through them only to realise that looking up the past is like looking up friends: we may knock at the door but it is chance that finds them at home. In both cases we make an entry, and from both discover that in the lottery of life and of literature a blank is the portion of nearly all expectation. Looking at the number on a draw-ticket, on the page of a diary, or on the door of a friend, we wonder how that was pleasure which is not to be had where it is alone to be found, and wonder moreover what virtue there can be in a habitation and a name when the face that was at once their hope and their remembrance has passed away.

It appears that he who would write a diary must pass over the finer furnishings of the day and the sumptuous upholstery of prose and of poetry, and learn to revel in the sawdust and shavings that are the first to be furthered into the fire and into forgetfulness. How easy it might have been is felt only when we are raking out the embers of memory, or when, in the vanity of retrieving what has vanished forever, we seek to assemble the smoke and to chase the scattered ashes on the wasting winds of past time. In the spirit of the prodigal we retrace our steps, but when we return at last to the old dwelling place the voices we knew have gone, the walls are agape to the wildness of the weather, and the storm is beating on the cold emptiness of the hearth. Well may we ask what are all the licences of life, the elaborations, the luxuries, the high optimacies of pleasure and the lengthened astonishments of style, when the first and familiar things, the tiny and trifled delights of other days are beyond recall? Pride is pleased to deny it, and yet it is a very late wisdom which learns that there is no passion so superb as cannot be lisped in the simple syllables of grief and gladness, and folly alone is left to enquire where in the order of the world is there a boast of pyramids without the downtrodden tribute of stones and the helping humility of hands, or where is there any nobility of landscape without the commonalty of the grass and the occasional grace of wild flowers? After all we may see into the depths of the universe from our own doorway and span the abysm of the spirit between the footstool and the fire.

Perhaps there is no darker alternative to writing a bad diary than to compose a successful classic, no more harrowing Hobson's choice than either to bury oneself alive or to be smothered perforce by friends. He who has escaped the pillory for his vices is cast into the stocks for his virtues: and having made the world the washpot of his wit and cast his shoe round every continental corner he is finally privileged to linger on in pensioned beggary as the refuge of schoolmasters and the affliction of boys. However cavalierly the Pegasus of today may course over the cosmic poles it must tomorrow sink down gravelled with classical gout, and despite the applause of contemporaries and the successive echoes of it through the generations, must enjoy no better fate than to be hustled off to the knacker's yard of the common critic or to provide the infancy of future ages with intellectual donkey rides on the sands of time. And what other obsequies has the poor beast than to be bullied into the corned beef of anthologies, to be shorn into upholstering the chairs of literature in higher schools, or to be flayed into such presentation leather bindings as bar all approach to the pages within? And what immortality may it hope for except to endure on in undusted editions and to be knocked down daily at unoutbiddable prices secondhand? Surely it is no distinction to have no more than that of being sold?

On returning to Bonn I made the admission that I had neither the temperament for a diary nor the skill for a classic, at least for such a diary as would interest others or for such classic as would content myself. I was pleased however to boast of patience, the unflinching patience that can plough a pavement, that can resolutely refuse every first impulse and dourly endure attendance on second thoughts. There is no prouder boast for it is a virtue of the universe, the virtue that doggedly adds drop to drop and grain to grain, and relentlessly allows the ages to leisure on from the infinites to infinity. The mind has indeed its moments but time has its eternities, and he who is resolved to wait may refuse failure. The bread that is cast on the waters returns, but only after many days.

Sometimes I have been in doubts myself, and when lingering overlong on elegancies of expression, on the lilts of language, and on the loveliness of alliteration, have wondered whether it is wise to venture everything on a breath, or to allow the hours to run to vagrancy in pursuit of failing forms and of evanescent voices. Of all our members the tongue is the least constant, and it is a precarious prosperity that comes of embarking the spirit on the instability of syllables and sounds. But where is there any foundation under the sun? And what is more idle than to raise hopes on duration in life, to speculate on favours above the universal fate, or to repine at the raft of earth when so hopelessly cast away on the waves of time? From lamenting our lot we come to lament the labour of it, to expect echoes louder than our speech, rewards transcending our deserts, and wisdom beyond our power to understand it. Gold is not to be gathered in the garden, and life will be found empty with much hesitation and dead with much delay by those who, persuaded of superior powers, take to the grander commissions, whether it be the quest of the precious stones or the cult of the precious style.

***